Twayne's Filmmakers Series

Warren French
EDITOR

The Golden Age of
French Cinema
1929–1939

Jacques Feyder and his assistant, Marcel Carné. Courtesy of Cinémathèque Française.

The Golden Age of French Cinema 1929–1939

JOHN W. MARTIN

BOSTON

Twayne Publishers

1983

The Golden Age of French Cinema, 1929–1939

is first published in 1983 by Twayne Publishers,
A Division of G. K. Hall & Company
All Rights Reserved

Copyright © 1983 by G. K. Hall & Company

Book Production by John Amburg

Printed on permanent/durable acid-free paper and bound
in the United States of America.

First Printing, October 1983

Library of Congress Cataloging in Publication Data

Martin, John, 1937–
The golden age of French cinema, 1929–1939

(Twayne's filmmakers series)
Bibliography: p. 146
Filmography: p. 150
Includes index.
1. Moving-pictures—France—History
2. Moving-picture plays—History and criticism.
I. Title. II. Series.
PN1993.5.F7M28   1983   791.43'75'0944   83-8557
ISBN 0-8057-9292-9

Contents

About the Author

A CINÉPHILE at a very early age, John Martin studied French and comparative literature at Yale and the University of Rochester. He worked for a time for Alfred Wagg Pictures, a documentary film company, as script writer and unit manager, making movies in Greece and Egypt on topics such as land reclamation in the Nile Valley. He has lived in France for four years, during which he became a devotee of the Cinémathèque Française. He has taught French, comparative literature and film at several universities. He has published articles on Greece in *Atlantic Monthly*, on Vietnamese refugees at American universities in *Change*, and on *Sir Gawain and the Green Knight*, Camus, García Márquez, and Wim Wenders in various periodicals.

Editor's Foreword

AT THE OUTSET of this multivolume history of filmmaking, it was my ambition to include a proper tribute to the Golden Age of French cinema, the decade from the international triumph of René Clair's *Sous les toits de Paris* at the beginning of the "talking picture" period in 1930 to Jean Renoir's flight from France and the fall of the Third Republic in 1940, following Renoir's ominously prophetic and bitterly controversial *La Règle du jeu.* I had long particularly regretted the absence in English (or in French) of any comprehensive account of this glorious era.

Clair's lighthearted fantasy and Renoir's dark allegory are two of the most written about classics of the medium; and a handful of other films from this decade of political chaos and artistic triumph in France appear on almost every list of the screen's masterpieces—Luis Buñuel's surrealist *L'Âge d'or*, Jean Vigo's *Zéro de conduite* and *L'Atalante*, Clair's *Le Million* and *À nous la liberté*, Renoir's *Boudu Saved from Drowning*, *Le Crime de M. Lange*, *Toni*, *Grand Illusion*, Marcel Carné's *Le Jour se lève*. Others equally worthy, however, have been generally forgotten—Marcel Pagnol's trilogy, *Marius*, *Fanny*, *César*, and his *The Baker's Wife;* Julien Duvivier's *Poil de carotte* and *Un Carnet de bal*, Abel Gance's *Beethoven*, Sacha Guitry's *The Story of a Cheat* and *The Pearls of the Crown;* Jean Benoit-Lévy and Marie Epstein's *La Maternelle*, Jacques Feyder's *Carnival in Flanders* (*La Kermesse héroïque*), and Anatole Litvak's *Mayerling*—although all of this distinguished dozen received high praise and extensive promotion in the United States.

Some of the finer French films of the decade have, however, scarcely been known or shown in this country—Duvivier's *David Golder*, *La Belle équipe*, and *La Fin du jour;* Feyder's *Le Grand jeu* and *Pension Mimosas;* Benoit-Lévy and Epstein's *Itto;* Jean Grémillon's *La Petite Lise*, *L'Etrange M. Victor*, and *Remorques;* Renoir's cooperative *La Vie est à nous;* and Andre Malraux's unfinished, suppressed, and nearly extinguished *L'Espoir.*

The influence of these films of France's golden decade upon film enthusiasts of my generation is incalculable. They introduced us to a concept of the screen as truly Abel Gance's "Seventh Art" that should take its place beside traditional painting, dance, and fiction. Although strict forms of film censorship existed throughout the world during the 1930s, French controls were more political—jealously aimed at preserving a national image—than moral, as in the United States and England, or ideological as in Germany, Italy, and Russia. Since moral and ideological straitjackets keep the arts simple-minded, childish, and escapist, it was only in France that the talking picture developed as a medium of sophisticated fare.

French films arrived in the United States in two waves during the 1930s. Although artists like René Clair had been reluctant to abandon silent film for the uncertainties of the sound medium, they were ironically responsible for the first really imaginative uses of the new resource. During the early 1930s when American talkies tended to be indeed "talky," as well as heavy-handed and slow-moving, film enthusiasts rejoiced in *Sous les toits de Paris, Le Million, À nous la liberté, Poil de carotte*, and *La Maternelle*, which long remained steady features of the first film repertoires in Manhattan and affluent suburbs.

My generation was principally influenced, however, by films shown locally, for example, in my native Philadelphia, where, in my high school years, the Europa Cinema was devoted exclusively to outstanding foreign movies. I recall vividly my first experience with subtitles at a much touted showing of Abel Gance's *Lucrezia Borgia*, or at least so much of it as survived Pennsylvania's specially strict censorship. Revisiting the film years later, I could see that it was shoddy in conception and execution, and I could well understand Gance's denunciation of the commercial films he had to make in order to finance a few cherished projects. At the time, however, his potboiler suggested a visual approach to history unhinted at by Cecil B. DeMille's edifying spectacles or Warner's stuffy biographies starring George Arliss.

Most important, the experience encouraged me to welcome *Mayerling*, which soon followed and set unprecedented attendance records for a foreign-language film, bringing even middle-class neighborhood theaters their first subtitled fare. This elegant tale of lovers doomed by autocratic powers exactly embodied the sense of helplessness induced by the long economic depression and the growing certainty of another world war. I have not seen *Mayerling* for years; it, too, may appear stilted and sentimental today. In its own time, however, it was a tragic romance without parallel in any other contemporary art form that gave us a sense of the evocative potential of film and the special superiority of French film.

No other foreign-language film enjoyed a similar response before World War II; but films like Sacha Guitry's *Story of a Cheat* and *The Pearls of the Crown* and the popular peasant fables like *The Baker's Wife, The Welldigger's Daughter* (1940), and *Harvest* provided both visual beauty and often raffish situations, still alien to our national cinema, that gave growing enthusiasts a new respect for the art of the film and the artfulness of French filmmakers.

The French "New Wave" has in recent decades largely obscured this earlier period, except for the work of Jean Renoir. (As earlier comments imply, we did not see much of Renoir during the 1930s, except for *Grand Illusion*.) It is pleasing that through the extensive retrospective program at the Museum of Modern Art in New York and elsewhere, a new interest in the forgotten and undiscovered masterpieces of the period is being kindled. John Martin's book is indeed a timely survey of this cinematic treasure trove. I have been fortunate to work with him for several years through a series of speculative blueprints in shaping a book that provides a perceptive introduction and guide to understanding this unique period in the early history of an art.

One feature of this book that may perplex connoisseurs of French film is the seeming slighting of Jean Renoir and the partial treatment of other prominent figures like René Clair and Marcel Carné. Since many excellent studies of Renoir have already appeared and since full consideration of his work would dominate an introductory survey that must fit the strict format of this series, we determined from the beginning that his work would be discussed only when it was essential to understanding the development of cinematic art in France during the 1930s and the growing tensions between the industry and political pressure groups as a result of the unflattering national image evolving in the film. We hope to include also a separate study of Renoir within this series.

This book needs also to be read in conjunction with our previously published studies of René Clair by Celia McGerr, Abel Gance by Steven Kramer, and James Welsh and Sacha Guitry by Bettina Knapp. Only key films by these four artists are discussed here where necessary to give an adequate sense of important developments in French film art.

The most serious problem with introductory studies of a rich period like the one considered here is that the demands of the works of a few outstanding masters usually obscures the contributions of gifted artists who deserve more attention than they have received. We determined, therefore, that the principal aim of this book would be to focus attention upon the achievements during the 1930s of those *auteurs* (though the term was then uncoined), especially Julien Duvivier, Jacques Feyder, Jean Grémillon, and Marcel Pagnol, whose works had not been adequately treated in English, and certain noteworthy films like

Benoit-Lévy and Epstein's *La Maternelle*, Jean Choux's *La Maternité*, Litvak's *Mayerling*, and Jean Delannoy's *Macao, l'enfer du jeu* by artists who had produced only a few relevant works—in order to provide an overview of the period and to place artistically and thematically significant films against a background of the French society of the age.

We hope that this book will help to bring these films back to our screens in many retrospective programs that will give us a broad concept of a unique period in film history at the same time that they entertain us in a way that only the classics of French cinema can.

W. F.

Preface

FOR MANY YEARS, the 1930s in France was known for a relatively small number of cinematic masterworks, principally by Renoir, Clair, and Carné. Yet the period produced over thirteen hundred feature films, the vast majority of which have received little or no critical attention. Recently, however, there has been a renewed interest in these neglected works, evidenced by a number of major retrospectives in Europe, Canada, and now in the United States, under the auspices of the Museum of Modern Art.

Like these showings, this study adopts a broad approach to the period. While not pretending to be comprehensive, it strives to strike a balance between well-known masterpieces and lesser-known movies which, for aesthetic, social, or political reasons, merit attention. In addition to discussing individual works, it seeks to provide a background of the era wide enough to afford insight into other films of the decade not touched on here.

As everyone who has worked in film criticism is aware, one of the great difficulties in undertaking a project of this scope is the availability, or, more often, the lack thereof, of the films themselves. Thus, accessibility has been an important factor in determining which movies I talk about. As a result, certain films and certain directors whom I would have liked to treat at length must await a time when this problem is less acute.

A study of this range is inevitably, to a significant degree, an *oeuvre de synthèse*, drawing often on the excellent critical and scholarly work of the past. For example, I found myself consulting Raymond Chirat's monumental filmography of the decade constantly. In the interests of readability, I have restricted footnotes to the identification of direct quotations. Translations, unless otherwise indicated, are mine. Those works which have been of unquestionable value to me are listed in the bibliography. The filmography is limited to those films available for rental in the United States (which accounts for the presence there of *La Grande illusion* which, because it has been dealt with so extensively elsewhere, I mention only in passing, as well as the absence there of other works which I analyze at length).

It has been the experience of Professor Michel Marie at the University of Paris III that the 1930s is the period that his film students prefer. I have found that American students respond positively to the decade as well. As the filmography indicates, an excellent selection of movies of the era is available from a variety of sources at a relatively modest rental fee, all of which makes these works particularly interesting to teachers of film in this time of ever-shrinking departmental budgets.

JOHN W. MARTIN

Acknowledgments

I WOULD like to thank Professor Warren French, who initially suggested the need for this study, for his enthusiastic and helpful guidance as the project took shape. I would also like to express my appreciation to the National Endowment for the Humanities, whose Summer Seminar Fellowship in Paris in 1979 made it possible for me to see a number of otherwise unobtainable 1930s films and to carry out valuable research which would otherwise have been impossible. In particular, I would like to express my thanks to Professor Theodore Reff, the director of that NEH seminar, for the example of his own perceptive visual analysis and for creating an atmosphere highly conducive to fruitful research. My thanks as well to Professor Michel Marie, who generously made the film collection at the Centre Censier available to me, who early on suggested that I expand the initial rather narrow scope of my project, who indicated at the outset the most valuable research materials available, and who provided me with a copy of his excellent article on *La Chienne,* on which my own discussion of the film draws heavily.

I would also like to thank Robert Daudelin and the staff of the Cinémathèque Québécoise, who received me most warmly in the cold Montreal winter, arranging for me to see numerous films at an awkward time, when they were being moved to new quarters. Special thanks, as well, to the Cinema Department of the Cultural Service of the French Embassy in Montreal for providing a number of screenings of difficult-to-obtain films and to the New York office of FACSEA for making available video cassettes of Armand Panigel's important television series on the history of French film. My thanks as well to the Cinémathèque Française for scheduling a number of private showings of films from its collection. I am especially grateful to Marie Epstein for granting me an interview and for her willingness to answer subsequent questions. My thanks as well to the Chicago office of Audio Brandon for making possible several days of private screenings. I am thankful also to Charles Silver and to the Museum of Modern Art for making possible my study of a number of essential films in the collection. My thanks also to Images,

Inc., for making available *La Femme du boulanger*. My special thanks to Sybille de Luze, Director of the Photothéque of the Cinémathèque Française, for providing on short notice stills from some of the less famous films of the period. Finally, I wish to express my gratitude to my wife, Professor Kathleen McNerney, whose continual advice and encouragement did much to bring this project to fruition and to whom I dedicate this book.

Chronology

1929   Hugon's *Les Trois masques*, the first French talkie; Paris premiere of *The Jazz Singer*.

1930   Clair's *Sous les toits de Paris*; Grémillon's *La Petite Lise*; Duvivier's *David Golder*; L'Herbier's *Le Mystère de la dame en noir* and *Le Parfum de la chambre jaune*; Buñuel's *L'Âge d'or*; de Limur's *Mon gosse de père*; Gance's *La Fin du monde*.

1931   Clair's *Le Million* and *À nous la liberté*; Renoir's *La Chienne*; Pagnol's *Marius*, directed by Alexander Korda; Gallone's *Ma cousine de Varsovie*; Raymond Bernard's *Les Croix de bois*.

1932   Duvivier's *Poil de carotte* and *La Tête d'un homme*; Renoir's *Boudu sauvé des eaux*; Pagnol's *Fanny*, directed by Marc Allégret.

1933   Vigo's *Zéro de conduite*; Benoit-Lévy and Marie Epstein's *La Maternelle*; Feyder's *Le Grand Jeu*; Hitler becomes chancellor of Germany.

1934   Vigo's *L'Atalante*; Feyder's *Pension Mimosas*; Pagnol's *Angèle*; Benoit-Lévy and Marie Epstein's *Itto*; Choux's *La Maternité*; Clair's *Le Dernier milliardaire*; Clair leaves France for London; 8 October, death of Vigo. Stavisky affair provokes bloody riots in the Paris streets and a failed right-wing coup d'état.

1935   Feyder's *La Kermesse héroïque*; Duvivier's *La Bandera*; Renoir's *Toni* and *Le Crime de Monsieur Lange*; Chenal's *Crime et châtiment*; Gance's *Un grand amour de Beethoven*.

1936   Duvivier's *La Belle équipe*, *L'Homme du jour* and *Pépé le Moko*; Guitry's *Le Roman d'un tricheur*; Renoir's *La Vie est à nous*; Pagnol's *César*; Litvak's *Mayerling*; Maurice Tourneur's *Avec le sourire*; Foundation of the Cinémathèque Française. Front populaire comes to power. Outbreak of Spanish Civil War.

1937   Renoir's *La Grande illusion;* Duvivier's *Un Carnet de bal;* Grémillon's *Gueule d'amour;* Pagnol's *Regain;* Guitry and Christian-Jaque's *Les Perles de la couronne.*

1938   Carné's *Quai des brumes;* Grémillon's *L'Etrange M. Victor;* Christian-Jaque's *Les Disparus de Saint-Agil;* Renoir's *La Bête humaine;* Chenal's *L'Alibi;* Gleize's *Légions d'honneur;* Pagnol's *La Femme du boulanger;* Duvivier's *La Fin du jour;* Pabst's *Le Drame de Shanghai,* Munich accords.

1939   Carné's *Le Jour se lève;* Renoir's *La Règle du Jeu;* L'Herbier's *L'Entente cordiale;* Delannoy's *Macao, l'enfer du jeu;* Lacombe and Mirande's *Derrière la façade;* Malraux's *L'Espoir* (first public showing 1945), Grémillon's *Remorques* interrupted by the war, completed in 1940, first shown in 1941.

1940   After several brief trips to Italy, Renoir leaves France for Hollywood. Capitulation of France and formation of Vichy government.

1

Introduction: The Silent Era

FRANCE HAS a long and distinguished cinematic tradition reaching back to the very roots of the medium. In 1895, Louis Lumière gave the first public projection of motion pictures, showing short films he had made of simple events such as the arrival of a train in a station, and using equipment of his own invention, the *cinématographe*. The company he formed with his brother Auguste did pioneer work in the field of the documentary, both distributing and filming on a world-wide basis. Their efforts were complemented by those of George Meliès, a magician turned *cinéaste*, who, in films such as *Le Voyage dans la lune* (1902), introduced movies to the realm of fantasy. Early in the century, both Charles Pathé and Léon Gaumont built international production and distribution empires.

L'Assassinat du duc de Guise (1908) by Le Bargy and Calmettes made a profound impression on D. W. Griffith and later Carl Dreyer. Both Gaumont and Pathé excelled in the genre of the serial and their productions packed houses in both Paris and New York. Probably the most inventive practioner of this form was Louis Feuillade, whose heroes were often criminals. *Fantômas* (1913–14) was much admired by Apollinaire and Max Jacob for its visually imaginative and lyric qualities. For the young future Surrealists, André Breton and Louis Aragon, *Les Vampires* (1915–16) embodied the most remarkable poetry of the time.

Unfortunately, World War I dealt a devastating blow to this flourishing film industry. During the 1920s, although France continued to produce interesting cinematic work, it was no longer able to command the same international preeminence. Surrealists like Marcel Duchamps and Man Ray carried out interesting experiments in the medium that

Charles Boyer and Danielle Darrieux, the elegant, starcrossed lovers of Anatole Litvak's Mayerling. *Courtesy of Cinémathèque Française.*

19

made France the leader in noncommercial avant-garde film. Directors like René Clair, Marcel L'Herbier, Jacques Feyder and Abel Gance all made films of individual importance. Clair's *Un chapeau de paille d'Italie* (1927) remains a masterpiece of comedy; L'Herbier, in such pictures as *L'Inhumaine* (1924) and *L'Argent* (1928), sought to develop a personal visual language; Feyder in *Crainquebille* (1922) created a stunning portrait of Paris which was much admired by Griffith; and Abel Gance in *La Roue* (1921–24) and *Napoléon* (1925–27) combined an extreme lack of measure with an extraordinary technical and visual imagination, lashing his camera to the back of a horse and plunging it into the sea from atop a cliff to capture the fever and tension of pursuit, and projecting certain episodes onto a triple screen. Nonetheless, the French could not match, on an international level, the consistently high quality of German expressionist and Russian feature films of the period.

At home, the industry had yet to regain its health. In 1925, 70 percent of the movies shown on the French market were made in America. In 1928, L'Herbier wrote "One cannot deny that 75 percent of the French people know the *cinématographe* does not exist."[1] At the close of the decade, two separate surveys showed that only between 7 and 15 percent of the public went to the movies, an audience drawn mostly from the poorer classes and intellectuals like the surrealists. Thus it was against a background of relative weakness in the French film industry that sound technology made its sudden, revolutionary appearance.

2

The Shock Waves of Sound

IN 1929 Abel Gance was in the midst of making *La Fin du monde,* which he later claimed would have been his best film, when a bomb from America exploded. It proved to be a very noisy one and it came from Warner Brothers, a small, new, and nearly bankrupt Hollywood studio. The company had gambled its remaining assets on the patent rights to Vitaphone, a system for making talking movies. Its first sound production, *The Jazz Singer* (1927), was a phenomenal international success, making the firm not only solvent but preeminent in the industry.

The advent of sound, so fortuitous for Hollywood, threw the French cinema into a state of disarray, illustrated by the fate of *La Fin du monde.* At first Gance tried to salvage his carefully composed scenario by simply adding sound to it, but he soon realized that he would have to discard much of the footage already shot and begin afresh. Unfortunately, he also had to contend with a producer who had no conception of the technical and financial problems involved in such a thorough transformation. Unable to get the money he needed to do the job right, Gance, in despair, washed his hands of the entire undertaking. Needless to say, in his eyes, the final result fell far short of its potential.

Ironically, the French had in their possession the scientific know-how that could have allowed them to lead the way into the sound era. Since the turn of the century, Léon Gaumont, one of the pioneers of the French movie industry, had sporadically pursued efforts to perfect a sound system based on phonograph records, not unlike Vitaphone. Another French inventor, Eugène Laste, had mapped out a method of recording a soundtrack alongside the image, directly on film. What the two men lacked was sufficient financial backing. In France talking pictures tended to be looked upon as a gimmick, a passing fad which would never exert a strong influence on the development of the cinema.

Nadia Sibirskaïa (Lise) and Julien Bertheau (André) say good-
night chastely outside her hotel in Jean Grémillon's La Petite
Lise. *Courtesy of Cinémathèque Française.*

The vast possibilities of the concept never captured the vision or the greed of the notoriously conservative French investment community. Laste's technique never made it off the drawing board, and although Gaumont worked out another process in conjunction with two Danish engineers, his impact on the commercial market was limited.

The Jazz Singer made its way slowly to French shores, finally premiering in Paris in 1929. Although it was not even a full-fledged talkie or a film of particularly high quality, the effect it had on Parisien audiences was electrifying. As in New York and London, it played to packed houses. It was followed by enough movies of greater merit like *Broadway Melody* (1929) and *Hallelujah* (1929) to make it clear that sound was here to stay.

As the public clamored for more talkies, French theater owners found themselves in a quandary. The cost of converting to sound projection equipment was extremely high, running from $30,000 to $100,000, depending on the size of the hall and the brand purchased. To equip a studio for audio recording ran as much or more. Since sound production was also at least three times more expensive than the making of silent films, French producers shied away from undertaking the higher cost of a talkie which could only be shown in comparatively few theatrical outlets. Carl Dreyer wanted to make *La Passion de Jeanne d'Arc* (1928) as a sound film, but could not get his French producers to bankroll him to go to London, where audio recording studios had already been set up. Although by the end of 1929 nearly one half of the 20,500 movie houses in the United States were equipped for sound, the changeover in France had scarcely begun. Yet the initial novelty of talking pictures in English had worn off and French spectators were demanding movies with French soundtracks. For a time, the French cinema was caught in an unusually vicious circle.

It was the Americans and the Germans who moved aggressively into the French market to bring about the changeover to sound. Although numerous audio systems were available, most French theaters elected to convert to RCA or Western Electric or the Tri-Ergon process owned by the German firm Tobis-Klangfilm. On the production end, in October 1928 Paramount set up studios in Joinville, which were equipped by Western Electric. Tobis fitted out its own studios at Epinay, along with those of Eclair at Epinay.

In order to stave off this foreign invasion, the major French companies retrenched and merged. Gaumont joined with Aubert to form Gaumont-Franco-Film-Aubert and Pathé combined with Rapid-Film to become Pathé-Natan. Despite this effort, neither firm was to make it intact through the decade, a harsh testament to the havoc the arrival of sound caused initially in France.

The Quarrel of the Ancients and the Moderns

The slowness of the French business community to adapt to the new world of sound was paralleled by the artistic reservations of a number of filmmakers who, during the 1920s, had been striving to evolve a cinematic language based on the expressive qualities of the image. Like Chaplin, von Stroheim, Eisenstein, and Murnau, René Clair and Marcel L'Herbier did not at first look upon talking pictures as a great leap forward. They felt that the silent cinema represented a unique art form, the only one developed by Western civilization, ideally suited to the needs of the twentieth century and just beginning to realize its extraordinary potential.

For Clair and L'Herbier, silent films were capable of creating a visual rhythm akin to that of music. Freed from the restraint of logic, they could transport the spectator into a realm of dreams completely divorced from ordinary reality. At the same time, they were totally international, a visual Esperanto with the power "to move the crowds of the entire world."[1] With dialogue, all these special qualities were sacrificed.

Clair also realized that talking films would require dialogue that could be readily understood by the least sophisticated members of the audience, drastically reducing their range of expression. He also foresaw that producers would set about adapting whatever play they could get their hands on, with little regard for quality, because it would be cheap and easy.

Marcel Pagnol adapted a diametrically different point of view. A playwright, whose *Topaze* had been a tremendous success on the Parisian stage, he saw *Broadway Melody* in London and was so impressed that he decided to abandon the theater in order to devote himself entirely to the cinema. He realized at once the great advantages sound production offered a dramatist. He could make multiple, lasting copies of his work, acted by the best cast available, through which he could reach out into the provinces, simultaneously touching audiences in Strasbourg, Poitiers, and Lyon, to say nothing of Montreal, in a way that a theatrical troupe could never hope to do.

Pagnol referred to silent film as a minor art and declared it dead. He announced a similar demise for the theater, which he said must be reinvented through talking movies. The cinema had indeed been considered by many as a poor relation to the other arts. Pagnol's pronouncements touched a sensitive nerve in Clair and a brisk polemic developed between them which was echoed in the press, where almost every day an article appeared either for or against sound.

Since Pagnol had never had any direct experience working in the cinema, he might perhaps have been more diplomatic in setting forth his views, which were the result of unbounded enthusiasm rather than malice. In the heat of the moment, their two positions seemed to represent irreconcilable opposites. In retrospect, the whole argument seems to have been founded on mutual misunderstanding. In any case, their theoretical differences resolved themselves in practice. Clair, who had been ready to abandon the cinema the first time he saw *The Jazz Singer*, went on to become completely reconciled not only to sound but to dialogue as well, as the years he spent working successfully in Hollywood demonstrate. Pagnol progressed rapidly from simply filming plays to the productions of works in which, with the collaboration of Jean Giono, the countryside as well as the people of his native Provence assumed an increasingly major role, making him one of the most important precursors of Italian neo-realism.

The Earliest French Talkies

The first, fully integrated, French sound production was André Hugon's *Les Trois masques* (1929). Since, in the absence of the necessary technical equipment, it could not be made in France, it was shot in the Twickenham Studios in London. Based on a play by Charles Méré, the filming took two weeks. Its soundtrack left much to be desired. The slightest noise was often magnified to the point where it drowned out the dialogue, and the voices of the actors were distorted. Yet, despite these obvious deficiencies, unavoidable given the unsophisticated state of audio recording, the film did lend some cinematic qualities to its theatrical source. It succeeded in creating the lively atmosphere of a village festival through the music, the laughter, the rhythmic steps of the dancers, and the shouting and the singing of the revelers. Other noises, such as the clucking of a hen, a storm, and, above all, the extraordinary novelty of hearing water flowing from a faucet into a sink, delighted audiences.

The first talking picture filmed in France was L'Herbier's *L'Enfant de l'amour* (1930), based on a play by Henri Bataille. Although it was a subject that appealed to L'Herbier, who had been planning for several years to make a silent version, the conditions under which he had to shoot the sound adaptation were, in a word, appalling.

It was produced by Pathé-Natan, whose Joinville studios had just been hastily equipped with RCA's Phototone system which, like its competition, was still in a somewhat rudimentary stage of development. The technicians had been hurriedly and inadequately trained. The camera, which made an undesirable grinding noise, had to be enclosed in a soundproof, cumbersome booth, so that the microphone, which, unlike those of today, had no directional selectivity, would not pick it up.

According to L'Herbier, "It was a masquerade. Arménise, our camera-man, couldn't get any fresh air inside the cabin and was covered with big drops of sweat. The sound was recorded by bulky microphones that weighed nearly fifty [*sic*] kilos, suspended in the air so precarious-ly that they fell on people's heads! The film suffered from all that, of course. . . ."[2] These were trying circumstances for a director who, during the silent era, had been accustomed to working in white gloves.

To overcome the linguistic barrier that dialogue automatically raised, it was customary to produce separate versions of each film in different languages. When it came time to shoot the German version of *L'Enfant de l'amour*, the situation became even more vaudevillesque. The French cast continued to play the roles, but without making a sound, pretending to speak words they did not know. The actual lines were delivered by German actors hidden under furniture or concealed be-hind screens just outside the range of the camera. It is not surprising that the synchronization fell short of the mark and the acting was, to say the least, extravagant.

"Babel-sur-Seine"

To justify the vast expense of equipping for sound, studios had to produce a substantial quantity of films as quickly as possible. No organi-zation was more adept at meeting this need than the Paramount studios at Joinville, where René Clair's worst fears became a reality. It was actual-ly a movie factory which operated twenty-four hours a day, completing feature-length pictures in multilingual versions in less than two weeks. *Magie moderne* (1931), for example, which was also called *Télévision* and contained sequences in Technicolor, was made in nine languages, in-cluding Dutch, Polish, and Czech. Paramount used the same sets, but hired separate casts of actors and actresses to perform in their native tongues. The corridors of the studio were filled with the native speakers from so many different countries that Henri Jeanson christened the establishment "Babel-sur-Seine" (Babel on the Seine).

The outfit was run by a cigar-smoking American named Bob Kane, who, although he had been in France for some years, spoke virtually no French, and who had a flag raised when he arrived at the studio and lowered when he left. It was said that when Bob Kane was looking at rushes of films in progress, he got very nervous if no one on the screen was talking.

Most of the Paramount scripts were taken from the vast repertoire of clever but shallow farces that, since the turn of the century, had been the mainstay of the *théâtre de boulevard*. These were performed by a polished troupe of veteran stage actors who, working together frequently, delivered the dialogue with disarming ease, improvising effortlessly when necessary and requiring little or no direction. Since the camera was usually quite stationary, the task of the director lay in filling in the gaps between scenes and acts. If the story took place on a train, for example, exterior shots of tracks, railroad cars, stations, telephone poles, and snatches of countryside sweeping by would provide the necessary transition. At the same time, they would furnish the work with a cinematic veneer while also giving the impression that the plot was moving along briskly. Christian-Jaque, who had done the decor for *Les Trois masques*, became particularly adept at this work, and many young directors, like Marc Allégret and Claude Autant-Lara, served their apprenticeship at Paramount.

However, the production of multilanguage versions proved far less profitable than had been projected. Toward the end of 1931, the technique of dubbing had improved enough in quality and had become sufficiently inexpensive to provide a viable alternative. Paramount, devastated financially by the effects of the depression, stopped producing original films in French and converted the Joinville studios into a dubbing center for Hollywood.

Le Cinéma de Boulevard

With very few exceptions, Paramount's entire output was eminently forgettable, but the studio was by no means alone in bringing frivolous stage fare to the screen. During the silent era, as has been noted, the cinema drew its audience mainly from two sectors of society, the poorer classes and the intellectuals. The bourgeoisie tended to prefer the theater and to ignore the movies.

Sound production changed all that. The cinema suddenly became respectable, attracting a large segment of the theatergoing crowd. All at once, stage directors who before had been considered lacking in visual sense discovered their services to be in great demand. Seasoned veterans of silent films like Henri Fescourt found themselves in the distressing position of having to prove their directorial talents all over again. Actors adept at delivering dialogue had little trouble finding movie work, while some of the most successful silent film performers fell by the wayside. Ivan Mosjouskine, one of the heartthrobs of the 1920s, never overcame the handicap of a heavy Russian accent.

These new spectators hoped to enjoy at the cinema just the same sort of entertainment they were accustomed to at the theater. To please them was to ensure success, so producers wanted to make movies with an atmosphere in which theatergoers would feel comfortable. This meant glamorous sets; elegant hotels; apartments with chic, modern furniture;

social receptions; fancy dress balls; and dance halls, if possible with jazz bands. Not all films had to have all these accoutrements, but they did need to set a luxurious tone and have a fashionable style. Two pictures which met these requirements with ease were Jean de Limur's *Mon gosse de père* (1930) and Carmine Gallone's *Ma cousine de Varsovie* (1931).

Mon gosse de père concerns Jérôme, a middle-aged Parisian man-about-town, who marries a young woman. Although he is an architect, he has never practiced his profession and returns from his honeymoon flat broke. Only then does it occur to him to try his hand at architecture, but he proves hopeless at business. The arrival of a son from America, Stanley, whose existence was hitherto unsuspected, saves him from further financial embarrassment. It is a bit awkward for Jérôme to explain the new member of the family to his wife, but Stanley soon tranforms him into a successful American-style businessman.

Adapted from a play by Léopold Marchand by the author and de Limur, the film presents itself as pure diversion, exemplified by the joke played on Jérôme at the outset, when he comes into the train station in Paris. He and his bride had hoped to slip into town unobtrusively. Not a chance. A little band is on the platform, ostensibly to greet an Arab prince, for whom they execute a lively fanfare. Then the musicians turn their full attention on the newlyweds, striking up a funeral march as they trail the embarrassed couple along the platform. This unanticipated reception has been arranged by Jérôme's friends, a witty divertissement with sound as the central element. The motif of music runs through the movie with a trombone blasting forth later in Jérôme's kitchen and a guitar strumming a romantic tango in the wee hours of the morning.

Mon gosse de père, a work whose conception remains essentially theatrical, continues to be entertaining even now by virtue of a masterly performance by Adolph Menjou as Jérôme. He radiates a uniquely French continental charm, which is heightened by his formidable reputation both on and off the screen as a ladies' man. Luis Buñuel, in the Spanish avant-garde review *La gaceta literaria hispanoamericana*, describes Menjou humorously as a nonliterary but very photogenic Don Juan and likens the power of his famous moustache, which in the film is seen frequently in close-ups, to the song of the sirens.

Jérôme's son Stanley serves as the perfect foil to set off Menjou's diffident urbanity. Stanley speaks with a horribly flat American accent, and his manners are as uncut as Jérôme's are polished. With his horn-rimmed spectacles, Stanley bears a curious resemblance to Harold Lloyd. Savagely sharp in business, he is in all other respects as relentlessly naive as his father is suavely sophisticated.

The world in which Jérôme moves is one of carefree elegance, of champagne cocktails, smoking jackets, and manicures. It is perfectly normal, perhaps even necessary, to sleep until noon and to drink champagne while taking a bath. The decor provides an appropriately sumptuous setting for this aristocratic life-style; furnishings are modern, elegant, and expensive, whether in the apartment salon or a luxurious nightclub.

Ma cousine de Varsovie unfolds within the same upper levels of society and concerns the visit of a Polish cousin, Sonia, to Archibald, a French banker. Archibald's wife is having an affair with Hubert, and to break this relationship up, Archibald asks his cousin to seduce Hubert. But Archibald himself falls in love with her, while she develops a real interest in Hubert. In the end, Archibald's wife, Lucienne, wins Hubert's affection back and Sonia leaves disappointed.

The film is an adaptation of a contemporary stage success by Louis Verneuil, who contributed many similar scenarios to the cinema during the 1930s. One of the collaborators on the screenplay was Henri-Georges Clouzot who specialized in transferring such light theatrical confections to the screen before he began making his own darker, more tortured works during and after World War II.

It was the play which launched the Parisian career of Elvire Popesco, and she re-creates the role of Sonia in the film, utilizing to the fullest the exotic appeal of her Romanian accent. From the outset, sound plays an important part in establishing her as a formidable and charismatic personnage. She arrives at Archibald's country domain in a flourish of frenetic speed and noise, tooling down the country road in a snazzy roadster, honking the horn and scattering startled geese and pigs from her path, amid much oinking and squealing. Later in the movie there is piano playing, singing, rifle shots, and much dialogue, some of which is addressed directly to the audience.

Mon gosse de père and *Ma cousine de Varsovie* have a number of characteristics in common, from which it is possible to abstract certain essential elements of the genre. First, although the people portrayed are rich, the work they do is not treated with any importance. Jérôme loses his first potential client, a rich developer sent to him by a friend, because he is discovered fooling around with party hats and noisemakers when the man arrives to discuss the job. Archibald is a banker, but he could just as well be an industrialist, a politician, or a notary, so quickly is his occupation eliminated from the film by the doctor who advises him to take a rest. Presumably the affairs at the bank run smoothly in his absence. The only people who treat work seriously are the lackeys who serve champagne and the ingenuous, socially dense American, Stanley.

In the end, idleness seems much to be preferred. How better to enjoy the sumptuous decors like Archibald's chateau? Hubert, on perpetual vacation, seems to reside there permanently, and his only worry is the unexpected arrival of Archibald from Paris for an extended stay, which can only put a crimp in the enjoyment of his love affair with Lucienne. Actually, Hubert is quite put out with his host, whose surprise visit to his own home Hubert considers to be rather bad form. It is particularly so since what really counts in this social setting is to behave at all times with *politesse*, always to observe certain social conventions—especially when someone is having a fling with your wife.

Other layabout types are needed for secondary roles: "to furnish this universe of lace and porcelain, a few sons (and daughters), no longer very young but as lazy as ever, who have never worked in their life and whose only preoccupation seems to be to make sure that their dinner jacket is well pressed and that their allure fits their amorous designs."[3] In their world nothing must ever be taken too seriously, a faux pas they are in no danger of committing. Thus, in *Ma cousine de Varsovie* a small peasant revolt takes place in the atmosphere of an operetta, completely trivialized.

These films and so many like them from the period appear on the surface to be pure entertainments, to have nothing to say. Yet they are by no means so innocent. They do have a message, an extremely conservative one: that the wealthy somehow deserve to be very rich, that even their arrogance and vacuousness is charming, that society is quite fine the way it is, and that no criticism is either necessary or appropriate.

For a director like Alberto Cavalcanti, interested in exploring the vast new possibilities of sound, the *cinéma de boulevard* could prove an unbearably stultifying way of earning a living.

I made French and Portuguese versions of American films at Paramount studios in Paris. I made about five or six of these films. After Paramount, I made a series of French comedies, which were awful, not only because they were talkies, but because they were sort of "boulevard talkies" in which people went from bed to table to supper and then back to bed. I was sick and tired. I had done four or five of these comedies and had signed for one more and then I didn't have the courage to go on. So I did what I have done many times in my long life. I said I was sick and I came to London to recover.[4]

There, as part of John Grierson's documentary team, he went on to do some imaginative experiments with sound, like *Night Mail* (1936).

Cinematic Sound

When the talkies first came to Hollywood, it, too, went through a period when filmed theater reigned supreme. At the same time, a small number of directors like Vidor, Lubitsch, Milestone, and Marmoulian began making films which utilized sound creatively rather than slavishly. Similarly, in France several veterans of the silent era, notably Julien Duvivier, Buñuel, Clair, and Jean Grémillon, began to investigate ways in which sound could expand the expressive possibilities of the cinema.

David Golder.   During the 1920s, Duvivier had established a reputation as a competent craftsman. When talking pictures first appeared, Duvivier's initial reaction was decidedly negative. Yet his first experience working with sound, *David Golder* (1930), exhibited such a seemingly effortless mastery of the new technology that it established Duvivier as a major director, and its star, Harry Baur, who was to remain Duvivier's favorite actor throughout the decade, as a top box office draw.

The film, adapted by Duvivier from a contemporary, best-selling novel by Irène Némirovsky, tells a story reminiscent in theme of *King Lear* and *Le Père Goriot*. David Golder is a rich, Jewish entrepreneur who idolizes his daughter, Joyce, and detests his wife, Gloria. Joyce is keenly interested in his money but cares nothing about him. She does, however, hypocritically play the devoted daughter and it is in order to provide her with the wealth she needs to marry a worthless prince that Golder swings his last, fabulously lucrative business deal, an agreement with the Soviet government. He dies on the way back from Russia, leaving his fortune to Joyce.

Duvivier had never become involved in the search for a uniquely visual film vocabulary that had preoccupied Clair and L'Herbier during the 1920s. He viewed the cinema primarily as a means of expressing dramatic action, so for him the transition to sound was, from the theoretical standpoint, far less traumatic. In *David Golder* he found a way to achieve a near-perfect balance between the skills he had acquired during the silent period and the exigencies of audio reproduction.

Many shots, for example, the striking views of Biarritz and the Basque coast, Duvivier took as if the entire film would be mute. In this way, at a time when sound engineers insisted that the camera remain virtually stationary, he was able to continue the kind of probing, subjective, fluidly graceful photography that characterized the best of Murnau's earlier movies. Yet he did not carry this technique too far, leaving much of the silent footage, which he realized would destroy the film's delicate equilibrium, on the cutting room floor.

In the same way, when so many other films were drowning in a sea of verbiage, he kept the dialogue, which he wrote himself, clipped to the bone. The scene between David and Gloria—in which, eyeball to eyeball, their faces glistening with sweat, she tells him that Joyce is not really his daughter but the result of an affair with an old friend—builds to a gripping dramatic intensity. At other times more quiet moments, such as the rather abstract overhead shot of the deserted Bourse, provide an effective contrast to such highly charged confrontations.

Sound heightens the emotional power of the final scene when Golder dies on the ship on the way back from Russia. The man who has moved up from the Polish ghetto to become a millionaire passes away surrounded by Jewish emigrants but really alone, with the image of his beloved but ironhearted daughter before his eyes, the singing of beautiful Hebrew chants in the background.

David Golder in certain respects anticipates *Citizen Kane* (1941), looking behind the public persona of a rich and powerful figure of the business world and revealing hitherto unknown information about his private life. Money brings happiness neither to Golder nor Kane; nor does their success shield them from the misery of loneliness. The film also establishes for the first time the harsh, bitterly pessimistic tone that was to characterize much of Duvivier's best later work.

L'Âge d'or.   Buñuel's *L'Âge d'or* (1930) distinguishes itself by its openly abrasive atmosphere. This savage satire of society and its hypocrisy, which alienates people from their natural feelings, is not, strictly speaking, a sound production. It was shot as a silent film and the soundtrack was added later. However, it deserves mention because the audio portion is used in a most unusual way: to destroy rather than reinforce the illusion of reality within the work. The movie, which by choice does not have a coherent plot, concerns a man and a woman who are potential lovers but who are kept by the pressures of society from consummating their desire.

Buñuel, who was active in the surrealist movement, sought to free both image and sound from the restraints of logic, which he felt were as inhibiting to artistic creation as those of society were to passion. For example, at an elegant party at the chateau of a marquis, a rustic peasant cart with huge wheels, which seems to have been temporarily displaced from a Constable landscape, suddenly enters a hall filled with guests in formal dress. As it rolls slowly across the floor, the wheels make a loud, rasping, grating noise. Yet none of the distinguished visitors pays the slightest attention to this incongruous vehicle, which is transporting two drunken farm workers, except to move aside, so that it can continue its progress unimpeded.

In another sequence, the woman protagonist, who, like the man, remains mysteriously nameless, sits at her vanity table. In the mirror she sees not herself but a sky with clouds sweeping across it. The whistling of a strong wind fills the room, which not only propels the clouds across the mirror but ruffles her hair and the flowers in a vase at her side as well. In the background, the barking of a dog links her to her would-be lover. In the preceding scene, while being led through the streets in police custody, he has just aggressively confronted two dogs who bark at him from behind an iron fence.

Finally, the two meet again in a garden and embrace to music of Wagner's *Tristan und Isolde*, which is being played at an outdoor concert nearby. At one point, although they remain dressed and do not make love, the voice-over dialogue between them is that of two lovers in bed:

SHE: I'm cold.
HE: Cover yourself well with the quilt.
SHE: Turn out the light.
HE: No, leave it. I prefer to see you.[5]

The lines represent the fulfillment of their sexual desires through fantasy, while underscoring their complete frustration in reality.

It was for the opening of *L'Âge d'or* that the surrealists published their most famous manifesto. The film, which overtly attacks the Catholic church and the repressive standards of society, provoked a riot at its premiere in Paris, in which right-wing houligans shouted "Death to the Jews!" in the theater and slashed surrealist paintings exhibited in the lobby. The movie, which remains to this day an extraordinarily powerful work, was immediately censored in France, a ban which, to my knowledge, has never been lifted.

Sous les toits de Paris. The most stunning international success of the year was René Clair's *Sous les toits de Paris* (1930). After a rather lukewarm reception in Paris, the film was shown in Berlin, where in one day the receipts payed for the entire cost of production. It met with an enthusiastic reception in London, New York, Tokyo, and Buenos Aires, as well demonstrating that the French cinema was still capable of competing with Hollywood on equal terms. The movie relates the story of a street singer, Albert, who falls in love with Pola, a young Romanian. Just as their romance, after the usual misunderstandings and false steps, is about to flower, he is accused of a theft engineered by his rival, a local heavy named Fred, and thrown in jail. While Albert languishes behind bars, his best friend Louis and Pola become lovers. In the end Fred is captured and Albert is released to return to his life as a *chanteur des rues*.

Clair began his career as an actor in the films of Louis Feuillade, the creator of the diabolically successful crime series, *Fantômas* and *Les Vampires*. Many of Feuillade's classic serials were set in Paris and developed a kind of poetry of the urban landscape—Musidora eluding capture, for example, by slipping out a window and escaping by crisscrossing the rooftops of Paris, silhouetted against a mysterious night sky. Clair continued to evolve this lyricism of the capital, as in the montage of chimney pots in *Entracte*. In *Sous les toits de Paris*, he utilizes the rooftop motif again as part of an evocation of a romantic, picturesque, poor quarter of Paris.

Much of the film's charm comes from Lazare Meerson's extraordinary sets which capture the essence of the little shops and bistros of a somewhat idealized section of town where ordinary people live. Like Feuillade, Clair takes us behind the facades of the buildings to show us how the city dwellers live their everyday lives. And like Feuillade, Claire exhibits a certain fascination with the criminal as well as the law-abiding element of urban society.

Since Clair had always shown a lively interest in music—the composer Eric Satie appears briefly in *Entracte*, for which he composed an original score—and equated the visual rhythm of silent films to that of a musical composition, it is not surprising to find that music plays a dominant role in the soundtrack of *Sous les toits de Paris*. The title song, which combines the twin themes of the rooftops and of penetrating behind the city facades, is the device by which Clair descends from the housetops to the pavement, where Albert is plying his trade as street singer. It is also the means by which, in a famous audio-visual pan shot, he moves lightly down the front of the building where Albert lives, entering the room on each story where, miraculously, all the tenants but one, an irascible killjoy, are singing the song. Shortly thereafter it provides the way by which Pola and Albert get to know each other, and their bittersweet love affair remains irrevocably intertwined with it to the point where, near the end when Albert accepts Louis and Pola's love, that is the tune he sadly plays on the bistro phonograph.

Clair frequently uses music to replace dialogue. Once, when Albert and Louis leave a dance and go out into the street, the accordion playing from inside follows them, louder than ever, drowning out the words of their quarrel. Clair keeps spoken lines to the minimum, in order to retain as much as possible the magic atmosphere of silent films. When Pola runs to tell Louis that Albert and Fred are fighting, we see her agitatedly describing the situation through the bistro window but we hear nothing. Similarly, a passing train blots out the noise as well as our view of the street scuffle. Once the train has gone by, Louis shoots out the street light and we hear but do not see the fight's continuation. This elaborate interplay of image and sound was probably suggested to Clair by a scene which he admired in *Close Harmony* (1929) of a dance-hall brawl which is heard but not seen. Music also supplants natural sounds. In the opening sequence, the rain falls silently, while the sound of raindrops is imitated on the background score.

At the same time, Clair occasionally makes clever use of dialogue. When Pola is obliged to spend the night in Albert's room because Fred has stolen her key, they argue about who will sleep in the only bed. They finally agree that they both will, and the lights go out. With the screen black, the argument starts right up again, with scuffling and protests from Pola, leaving us to imagine all that might be going on. They both end up sleeping on the floor on opposite sides of the bed.

The freshness of *Sous les toits de Paris* has paled somewhat over the years, but it remains an important picture because Clair, like Duvivier, succeeded in retaining full artistic control over filming at a time when most directors had relinquished it in large part to the sound engineers. Until the new equipment became more sophisticated, the word of these technicians was usually law. Almost all of them were either English or American and the French used to call them "nutcrackers" because they would arrive on the set on the first day and walk around snapping their fingers to test the acoustics. Inevitably, their verdict was "No good!" and they would insist that further measures be taken, such as hanging cloth on all the walls. They often decided not only where the microphone would be placed but the position of the camera as well. When Clair wanted to let the mike as well as the camera sweep down the side of the building in *Sous les toits de Paris,* he was told that the idea was impossible, that the camera could not be moved like that. He did it anyway and came up with one of the film's most striking sequences, in which the sound is flawless.

La Petite Lise.   Clair's interest in music and his fanciful use of it in *Sous les toits de Paris* coincided with a moment when the public's taste for filmed operettas, like *Le Capitaine* Craddock (1931) and *La Guerre des valses* (1933), was on the rise, a trend which certainly made acceptance of Clair's audio experiments easier. By contrast, *La Petite Lise* by Jean Grémillon is a film which ran directly counter to the preferences of most spectators in 1930, particularly those recently won over from the theater. It owes little to the stage in either style or technique and represents an ambitious attempt to develop the possibilities of sound for exclusively cinematic ends.

La Petite Lise tells the story of a convict, Berthier, in the prison colony of Cayenne who, for an act of courage, is unexpectedly pardoned. He returns to Paris and is reunited with his beloved daughter, Lise. She and her fiancé, André, desperate for money, unwillingly commit a murder, the blame for which Berthier shoulders to spare his daughter the hell of prison.

This simple, tragic melodrama unfolds in a way that prompted Henri Langlois, the founder of the Cinémathèque Française, to say "It was when I saw *La Petite Lise* that I forgot *Sous les toits de Paris* and stopped regretting the end of the silent era."[6] Langlois's deliberate opposition of the two works reflects a radical difference in the basic attitude of each director toward sound. Although Grémillon had made two silent feature films, *Maldone* (1927) and *Gardiens de phare* (1929), he looked upon the new technology positively, as being challenging and rich in potential. Unlike Clair, he was willing from the outset to adapt completely to it: "The talking film poses all over again the question of the construction of the drama, of its means of expression, of acting and editing. Almost none of the values acquired during the silent period can subsist, especially the shooting script and the editing. The talking film multiplies the means of direct action in the cinema."[7] *La Petite Lise* represents a bold initiative launched from this point of view, an attempt to strike out in new directions rather than to preserve the past.

Grémillon was even more intimately involved with music than Clair, having studied composition under Vincent D'Indy at the Schola Cantorum, played in a moviehouse orchestra accompanying silent films, and presented one of his early works, *Un tour au large* (1926), with a musical score which he wrote. Although in *La Petite Lise* music does not dominate the soundtrack as it does in *Sous les toits de Paris*, it nonetheless remains a major element.

Grémillon employs music principally to create the atmosphere and to set the psychological tone of a scene, frequently before the visual component of a sequence has appeared. The film begins with music, a heavy yet strangely resonant chord, struck while the screen is still black which gives the feeling of raw nerves vibrating. It is followed by a rhythmic ticking that is full of foreboding. A hypnotic Creole song with a heavy drumbeat then begins providing a background for the credits. The opening chord and the ticking presage ill fortune, while the Creole song suggests a distant, foreign, tropical setting, preparing us for the cheerless mood of the prisoners who must live far from home, lonely amid the forced companionship of the crowded dormitory with its plaintive graffitti of "Clichy" and "la petite femme" scratched on the wall. The tense chord and the ticking fit well with the implacable heat of Cayenne the claustrophobic feel of the smoky, cramped communal quarters, and the desolate look of the convicts, seen first from behind, their faces all but hidden behind their hats, anonymous with their shorn heads and colorless prison garb, their identities reduced to mere numbers by the penal system. The sentimental song the prisoners sing, which covers the rasp of a prisoner sawing through a bar, underlines their universal homesickness.

Later, when Lise and André enter the courtyard where the pawnbroker lives, a Semitic, prayerlike call hovers in the air. Heard once again when they are inside, it prepares us for the moneylender, who wears a skull cap and a beard, speaks with a Jewish accent, moves with slow, oily gestures, and drives a mercilessly hard bargain, a portrait which smacks of anti-Semitism.

At the movie's end, Grémillon uses music to underscore, by means of contrast, the psychological state of his characters. When an enraged Berthier, in the mistaken belief that André is a pimp who had led his daughter into prostitution, provokes a confrontation, it takes place in a Left Bank night club filled with exuberant dancers and lively swing music. The happy jazz stays constantly in the background when Lise gives her father a full explanation and he becomes reconciled with André, a counterpoint to the somber, depressed mood of the three, who talk together in a small adjoining room.

When Berthier leaves the nightclub to give himself up to the police, the music switches to the Creole mode, recalling the song with which the film opened. It joins with the rapid flashback of the penal colony— which is also a flash forward—to make clear Berthier's ultimate destination. He cannot, of course, hope for a second reprieve, and the weight of the prospect of living the rest of his days out in the inferno of that captivity, plus the shock of his daughter's role in the death of the pawnbroker, cause him to move with uncharacteristic slowness, almost like a sleepwalker, through the dancers, most of whom are now black. The camera lingers on one woman with a kerchief around her head, who has a particularly Creole air. The animated beat of the song, punctuated by handclapping, and the exuberant pleasure of the revellers sets Berthier, with his introverted somnabulent movements, completely apart. The high-spirited music hounds him all the way to the police station.

Grémillon stated that "a character who speaks does not interest me anymore than a motor, a siren, etc. . . ." and a variety of noises enriches the soundtrack of La Petite Lise. [8] A bell tolls at the beginning to bring the convicts in from work. A whistle marks the failure of the escape attempt of Berthier's friends. Lise lives in a room in L'Hôtel du Nord and we frequently hear the sounds of trains pulling in and out of the station. The chugging, whistling, and braking of the railway cars we never see brands the location as a place of transience and impermanence which fits not only with the life of a streetwalker that Lise leads but also with Berthier's tragically temporary return to Paris.

The woodworking shop where Berthier gets his old job back, together with a generous advance from his boss, is filled with the whine of saws slicing through boards. The loud, regular thudding of a machine reverberates throughout the entire establishment. The two sounds create an ambience of serious, hard but honest travail.

During the robbery, we hear but do not see the pawnbroker open his safe, while the camera concentrates on the faces of Lise and André, torn between resolve and hesitation. Nor do we actually witness the death of the moneylender. Originally planned as a gruesome bloodbath, it occurs off-camera. We only hear the thud of the vase which Lise brings down on his head. Then the camera reveals a grim still life of André's gun and the broken pieces of the shattered vase on the floor, through which a rivelet of blood begins to creep slowly. The sound of the doorbell, rung by another customer, pierces the air, terrifying them. As soon as they can, they hurry off without taking either the money or the watch which they were pretending to pawn and whose ticking links it to the similar portentous sound at the film's beginning. As they hurry through the placid courtyard under the watchful gaze of the concierge, the clip-clop of horses' hooves on the street outside underlines how the tranquil peacefulness of everyday life has abruptly changed for them and may never be the same.

The dialogue in *La Petite Lise* is straightforward and functional. Grémillon never accords it undue importance. At the beginning in the dormitory sequence, voices of the convicts form a part of the auditory background as they settle in for the night, lighting fires, playing cards. What they actually say is often blurred and of no matter; it is simply an integral part of the constant noise of cramped quarters.

Although he does not, like Clair, make a fetish of suppressing dialogue, Grémillon occasionally uses silence to effectively underscore intense emotion. When Lise and André go to a restaurant after the murder to establish an alibi, it happens that two of André's friends are seated in the nearly deserted dining room. André makes a point of going over to speak to them, leaving a terribly distraught Lise sitting alone at their table. André's conversation with the others appears as a pantomime in a mirror hanging on the wall beside Lise. Then the camera moves in to frame her face, tears running down her cheeks as she sits in silent misery, her eyes filled with fear and regret.

The end of the film passes in absolute quietude. Berthier, in a state of shock over the murder and the abrupt destruction of his recent good fortune, makes his way to the police station when the tolling of a bell, like the one in Cayenne at the beginning, suddenly cuts off the night club music. He enters the station, sits down, and begins talking to an officer. The conversation is completely inaudible but the nature of his sacrifice is clear. The camera draws slowly back, abandoning him to his fate.

Grémillon's investigations into the unchartered territories of sound, together with his choice of subject matter so far removed from the boulevard comedies and operettas which filled the screen, incensed his producer, Bernard Natan. Natan, a foreigner and a Jew, could also hardly have been enchanted with the stereotyped and offensive portrait of the pawnbroker. The head of Pathé-Natan was so furious that he told Grémillon he was finished at the studio in such a brutal way that Grémillon went outside and vomited against a wall across the street. It was not until the decade was drawing to a close and the content and style of films quite similar to *La Petite Lise*, aided by the charisma of Jean Gabin, were gaining a wide audience that Grémillon was once again able to make movies with a reasonable amount of autonomy.

Three Masterworks

In 1930 France turned out eighty talking pictures. The next year, the output of films more than doubled. While most of these aimed at commercial rather than artistic value, at least three stand out as masterpieces: Jean Renoir's *La Chienne* (1931), Clair's *Le Million* (1931), and Pagnol's *Marius* (1931), directed by Alexander Korda.

La Chienne.   Renoir, who had made seven silent movies, came into the sound era with the reputation of a director who worked slowly and required a large budget. Producers, put off by the higher cost of the talkies, tended to shy away from him, until he shot a mediocre farce by Feydeau, *On purge bébé* (1931), in a few days. In addition to a great deal of other bathroom humor, it featured for the first time the noise of a toilet flushing and was a hit at the box office, giving Renoir the chance to complete a more worthwhile project he had in mind, *La Chienne.*

Adapted from a contemporary novel by Georges de la Fouchardière, *La Chienne* recounts the amorous adventure of a cashier, Legrand. Stifled by his job and his shrewish wife, Adèle, he falls in love with a prostitute, Lulu. He sets Lulu up in an apartment but she only uses him to get money for her pimp, Dédé, who clearly has no real interest in her. Legrand becomes aware of her deception and kills her. Dédé is convicted of the crime and executed. Legrand, who has been lifting company funds to finance his romance, is fired and becomes a bum.

Having conclusively demonstrated his ability to use sound frivolously, in *La Chienne* Renoir utilizes it with considerable creativity. At a time of still primitive audio-recording equipment, when few directors were willing to venture outside the studio, Renoir shot numerous scenes in the street, using mattresses and blankets to help muffle unwanted sounds. The soundtrack is embellished with a variety of outdoor noises such as automobile horns and motors, a clock striking, the echoing of footfalls on the pavement, falling rain and rainwater gurgling in the gutter.

Interior sequences sometimes have a dense audible background as well, like the early banquet scene with its clinking glasses, the laughter and stag-party conviviality of the guests. Often sounds symbolize character, as in the scene of Legrand's return home following his first meeting with Lulu. It begins with two noises, first of a cuckoo clock, then of Legrand, vainly trying for a quiet entrance, knocking over his easel. The cuckoo represents the repressively rigid order, unsoftened by any warm emotion, which reigns in Adèle's life and which she attempts to impose on her husband. Awakened by the din he makes in the dining room, she immediately checks the time, then rails at him for coming home so late, when he was under orders to be back by eleven o'clock. The easel, on the other hand, is an indication of Legrand's dreamy, romantic, artistic nature, undoubtedly the most annoying way in which he holds out against her attempts to whip him into line. He has no studio, and the easel and paintings litter the otherwise impeccably bourgeois arrangement of the apartment. According to her, the other respectable inhabitants of the building make fun of him for his pictorial bent and she threatens to give all his canvases to the ragpicker if he fails to get rid of them himself. Although she commands him to hurry up and get to bed, slamming the door as she retires, the scene closes with him dallying over one of his paintings, a manifestation of his unwillingness to knuckle under.

The same kind of opposition governs another key sequence in the apartment, when Legrand pilfers Adèle's cache of money, loot he will spend on Lulu. The auditory background for the episode comes from another flat located across a courtyard. In it a little girl practices the piano, going over and over an exercise with limited proficiency. Does she have a genuine interest in music, in mastering the instrument? Or are piano lessons simply a means of adding tone and prestige to her education, of increasing her social graces? The tedious scales imbue the scene with a suffocatingly conventional, pretentious, middle-class atmosphere against which the theft stands out as a revolutionary act. Once he takes the money, the die is cast. He has irrevocably disrupted the bourgeois world of respectability in which he has been ensnared. To underscore this polarization, his larceny is carried out in complete silence, while, ironically, the mindless piano playing provides a kind of cover for his act of rebellion.

Renoir also uses songs to prefigure characters. At the end of the banquet, a phonograph record of a serenade by Torelli, one which at the time was popularly held to presage misfortune, is heard in snatches during gaps in the conversation. The lyrics are: "Come, night is falling / The breeze is enchanting / Come, you who are so sensitive to the cold. . . . A smile in your large eyes / Reveals to me a corner of the skies."[9] Janie Marèze, who plays Lulu, has big, round eyes and the romantic song clearly foreshadows the fateful meeting that will occur shortly.

The same little girl who plays the piano sings at her courtyard window a traditional French folksong, "Marlborough goes off to war." Adèle is constantly comparing Legrand to her first husband, Godard, who went off to war, only to vanish, presumably dead. Later in the film he resurfaces and tries to blackmail Legrand, who cleverly traps him into being reunited with Adèle, setting himself free to be with Lulu. Back at home from the café where he has set his coup in motion, under the portrait of Godard which still hangs in the dining room, he sings the folksong again: "Marlborough goes off to war / Doesn't know when he'll come back" (20). The clear connection between Godard and the august English general is tinged with a double irony. Adèle still thinks of him as an exemplary military man: "Yes, the adjutant. A real man! A hero! One of those brave men who went to their deaths in 1914 for loafers like you [Legrand]" (10). However, we know that the adjutant, who used to look so dashing on parade, is about to resurface, involuntarily, as a bum.

There is added irony in the fact that Legrand is about to desert Adèle and, like his predecessor, take off on the road to freedom. Yet in a society as unbending and oppressive as his, it seems that there is no way to go but down, and Legrand will also end up a hobo. Yet he is perhaps not entirely a failure. In the epilogue, when the two vagabonds meet again by chance, Legrand is at last his own man, at peace with himself and than he ever had been.

But before Legrand finds liberty, he finds Lulu in bed with Dédé and later, unable to stand her mockery of his love, he kills her. The death scene is set against the background of a street song whose words, harking back to the Torelli serenade, suggest Legrand at his most wildly romantic: "If I sing beneath your window / Like a gallant troubador . . . / Be kind, oh my beautiful stranger / For whom I have sung so often" (23). But the beautiful stranger is not kind to the gallant troubador. She laughs in his face until he silences her with a letter opener.

As in *La Petite Lise*, we do not see the actual murder. Several times during the argument the camera returns to the street singers, the third time slowly traveling up the facade of the building, stopping briefly to frame a black cat, the Baudelairian symbol of illicit sex. Finally it shows her dead body through the window, a grief-stricken Legrand hovering over it. The song remains in the background.

Dialogue also plays an important part in establishing both personality and social class. Michel Simon, who plays Legrand, is uncharacteristically taciturn in the early portion of the film. He frequently seems oblivious to the jibes of his colleagues or the harangues of his wife, which he barely bothers to counter. His expression is abstracted, as if he lives in his own introspective dreamworld. His body, too, is hunched, turned in upon itself. Later, as he begins to assert himself, his bearing becomes less cramped and he has a great deal more to say, until, in the epilogue, he displays the kind of physical and vocal freedom later to be seen in such wild eccentrics as Boudu and Père Jules. Thus the move from reticence to volubility marks the flowering of his suppressed temperament, as he gives it ever greater freedom of expression.

Renoir also carefully modified the diction of Janie Marèze, an opera singer who had just triumphed in the title role of Marc Allégret's *Mam'zelle Nitouche* (1931). Raised in a well-to-do family, her refined accent was all wrong for the role of a prostitute. The success of Renoir's efforts may be measured by the fact that in the film her intonation is perfect for the part. Renoir had no such problem with Georges Flamant, a real-life pimp who was type-cast as Dédé. His speech, naturally laced with Parisian slang, contributes to his downfall in the witness box. He is innocent, but his manner of speaking makes him seem guilty. A similar differentiation through speech patterns exists between the minor characters. For example, Legrand's boss speaks quite differently from Lulu's concierge.

Renoir's producer was expecting a frilly comedy. He was so exasperated by the relentlessly bleak tone of the rushes that he took legal steps to bar Renoir from the cutting room. Fortunately, he was unable to transform the movie into something more vacuous and was obliged to recall Renoir to do the editing. Janie Marèze was less lucky. Georges Flamant, in anticipation of a brilliant film career, like Dédé, bought himself a new car. When he took her for a ride in it, there was an accident in which she was killed.

Le Million.   In *Le Million* René Clair further refined and perfected the audio techniques he had introduced in *Sous les toits de Paris*. At a time when Grémillon and Renoir were working in a harshly naturalistic vein, Clair moved farther away from reality into his own special world of fantasy, with music serving once again as the principal element of sound.

The movie is about a young art student, Michel, who wins the national lottery but loses the winning ticket. It is in the pocket of a threadbare jacket which his girlfriend, Béatrice, gives away to a picturesque crook, le père la Tulipe, who needs a quick disguise to elude some cops who are after him. The hunt for the ticket reaches its climax during a performance at the Opéra-Lyrique. All ends happily as Michel, the ticket again in hand, becomes a millionaire.

Although Clair was vehemently opposed to unimaginatively filmed plays, he was by no means opposed to the theater. In *Un chapeau de paille d'Italie*, he had already made a free adaptation of a comedy by Labiche, utilizing only two of the five acts. *Le Million* is based on a vaudeville farce by Georges Berr and Michel Guillemaud, with which he took even greater liberties.

When Clair began working on the script and realized that what attracted him to the play was his old nemesis, the dialogue, he wanted to call the project off. But it was too late; his producer, Tobis, had already bought the screen rights. "I was obliged to continue and conceived the idea of re-creating the unreality of the vaudeville by replacing words with music and songs. I am delighted to have discovered this operetta formula where everybody sings except the main characters, and I began to envisage musical elements directly inspired by the action."[10] In the finished film there is a great deal of singing and very little dialogue. Music also often replaces natural sounds, as when Michel's erstwhile friend, Prosper, breaks a vase near the beginning.

Ballet, a closely related art, also plays a major role in *Le Million*. Clair had long been an ardent admirer of the dance, of Diaghilev's Ballet Russe and of the Ballet Suédois. He had also been quick to perceive its relevance to the cinema, the very essence of which is movement. He praised the rhythmic grace of *Robin Hood* (1922) starring Douglas Fairbanks: "Forget the plot. Judge *Robin Hood* as you would judge a ballet, a fairyland."[11] He goes on to place the work on equal footing with Victor Hugo's *La Légende des siècles*.

In *Le Million* characters sometimes step with stylized gait, like the gang of thieves led by le père la Tulipe, who professes a philosophy of theft similar to Robin Hood's. The group of Michel's creditors, all local shopkeepers, sing and, like a Greek chorus adapted to humorous ends, comment on the action, on occasion moving all together to the cadence of their singing. But the whole film is choreographed around the motif of the chase, which reaches back to the first golden age of French cinema, to the heyday of Louis Feuillade, whose serials were most often built around hot pursuit. Clair was also an old hand at the device, having used it to great effect in *Entracte* and *Un chapeau de paille d'Italie*. The creditors chase Michel, the cops pursue le père la Tulipe, and the two hunts overlap. Michel, Prosper, and Béatrice try to track down the elusive ticket. The pace of the film builds slowly, like a Marx Brothers' comedy, until all the elements—music, ballet, and the chase—converge in a frenetic climax during an evening performance of *Les Bohémiens* at the Opéra-Lyrique, where Béatrice works as a dancer.

Michel's shabby jacket has been acquired by the leading male singer in the opera, Sopranelli, as a part of his costume. The frenzied search for it, which now also involves the gang of le père la Tulipe, erupts onstage during the show. Michel finally gets his hands on the coat and is chased across the stage, through the wings and corridors by a swarm of people which now includes the crew of the opera house. Clair choreographs the spirited sequence like a ballet. Then, through the soundtrack, he introduces another element closely akin to the athletic nature of the dance. As the jacket passes from person to person, is dropped and grabbed by someone else, we hear the roar of a crowd, the whistle of a referee, and all the other noises of a real rugby match. Having disassociated image and sound, Clair links them by photographing a pile-up of pursuers, the equivalent of a rugby scrum, from a high angle, the perspective of a spectator in a stadium.

Clair also employs the device of a play within a play to satirize the artificiality of theatrical conventions. The opera performance features an enormous, pot-bellied Italian tenor (Sopranelli) and a blonde, Wagnerian soprano of equally formidable proportions, who are cast as lovers onstage but are bitter professional rivals offstage. The first time they meet in the film, they begin shouting at each other because one has kept the other waiting, an altercation which turns into a running quarrel.

Later, Michel and Béatrice, who have also been arguing, are trapped onstage when the curtain rises for a love duet between the two lead singers. Michel and Béatrice take refuge behind some props, but must remain silent. The only way they can communicate their genuine emotions is through the hackneyed lyrics of the song, which they pretend to deliver through pantomime, as the words are sung. In this way, Béatrice can tell Michel, "Yes, my despair is extreme / Nothing will console my heart / You do not love me, the one who loves you!" And Michel can answer, "Don't listen to your jealous heart / I love you and am at your feet." The scene ends with a reconciliation between both the characters in the opera and Michel and Béatrice. As both couples embrace, fake petals rain down on the stage. As soon as the curtain falls, the two singers start fighting with each other, again in pantomime, their insults drowned out by applause. When the curtain rises for a bow, they immediately reassume their stage personae of happy lovers. The enthusiastic clapping of the audience drives the curtain up and down several more times, while the singers switch back and forth between love and antagonism.

It is possible to see the embryo of this droll satire in a scene from *Showboat* (1929), one of two in the film which Clair singled out as remarkable. It, too, takes place on stage, utilizing the motif of a play within a play. An actor and actress recite their lines solemnly, while in an undertone declare their love to each other, setting up a date for after the show. Neither the audience nor the director, who is in the wings, imitating the chirp of a nightingale, can hear their whispers of endearment. "You can imagine what a clever director [Harry Pollard] did with the alternation of the affected declamation and the sincere whispering, the interchange of long shots and close-ups. Neither the silent cinema nor the theater could have created this effect."[12] Clair uses the idea in an original way, adding another couple and pantomime to the mix. In *Le*

Million, unlike Clair's first experiments in *Sous les toits de Paris*, the suppression of dialogue is no longer a somewhat negative end in itself. Here it forms an integral part of the most witty scene in the film.

Clair's use of the play within a play contains an additional satiric dimension. Michel and Béatrice exist within the framework of a shop-worn literary convention, the romanticized Bohemian life of the struggling artist, the very background of *Les Bohémiens* itself. Sopranelli immediately recognized Michel's jacket as the perfect costume for his role. Within this context it is fair to ask just how genuine the love between Michel and Béatrice can be. Clair is parodying not only the artificiality of the world of the theater, but his own use of that very artificiality as well.

The film ends, as it began, with music and dance brought together again, as the revellers celebrating Michel's good fortune sing and dance in the round, a finale of a type later to be used often by Frederico Fellini.

Marius.   Unlike the many eminently forgettable films churned out at the Joinville studios of Paramount, *Marius* (1931) stands out for its unusually excellent quality. To be sure, the conditions under which it was made were anything but typical. Pagnol held out for and obtained almost complete artistic control over the production. He wrote the dialogue and shooting script and was allowed to select the cast. He also supervised the actual filming. Authors were not held in high esteem at Paramount, and for one to acquire such power was indeed exceptional. But Pagnol developed a special relationship with the head man, Bob Kane, who brought Alexander Korda from Hollywood to direct the picture and authorized the construction of special sets which add considerable charm to the film's atmosphere, especially when compared to the bare, white ones of virtually all Paramount productions.

Needless to say, Pagnol engaged the same troupe of actors who had made the play such a resounding success and who had the experience of eight hundred performances under their belts. The degree to which the actors became identified with their roles is indicated by the fact that Charpin, who plays Panisse, came to be called Panisse in real life. On the first day on the set, a problem caused by the still-primitive sound equipment arose with the most important actor, Raimu. The engineer declared that it was impossible to record Raimu's voice. Korda asked if it really was completely impossible. The engineer said yes. Korda said "That's too bad." The engineer said "Yes, it's too bad for Monsieur Raimu." Pagnol intervened: "No, it's too bad for you, because Monsieur Raimu can't be replaced, but you can be," he said. The exchange made Bob Kane nervous and he told Pagnol, "Don't talk like that to that technician. He won't want to do any more work." Apparently a solution was found, because the dialogue in the film was recorded with exceptional fidelity and Raimu's performance as César was one of the strongest elements in the film.

A clear soundtrack was essential because so much of the movie's atmosphere comes from the heavily accented speech of the actors like Raimu. In addition to the intonations and speech patterns of the south of France, the dialogue contains a fair amount of words from Provençal and marks the first time that language was spoken on the screen. For example, Aunt Honorine, when she gets angry, vents her spleen in Provençal.

Marius takes place in the old port section of Marseilles. A young man, Marius, dreams of faraway places. He is in love with Fanny and has an affair with her. Against his father's advice, he takes a job on a ship and sails away. Most of the action is set in the Bar de la Marine, which Marius's father, César, owns, and the film has been criticized for sticking too closely to the play.

It does have a certain closed-in quality, and it is true that Korda did not utilize the potential of the cinema to open the narrative up as much as he might have. Pagnol was initially skeptical about Korda and Raimu, who directed the actors in the stage production, was furious at the idea of a Hungarian directing a movie about Marseilles. But Korda brought to the project a deep respect for the text and he did not take a single shot without first explaining to Pagnol what he was doing and why. This close collaboration resulted in a film that is completely faithful to the original play and also allowed Pagnol, who had no technical cinematic experience, to learn a great deal about the making of a motion picture.

Korda did use a limited number of exterior shots to suggest the ambience of the old port. The film opens with an overview of Marseilles, the docks and streets, and Korda cuts from time to time to shots of the masts of boats in the harbor. He also uses the lighthouse at the edge of the bay to mark the passage from day to night. To these visual images are added sounds which evoke the maritime setting: the whistles of ships, the clanking of their iron chains, and the cries of sailors hailing other ships. Marius, who works as a waiter in his father's waterfront café, knows the sound of every boat whistle by heart. When he hears one, he recognizes which boat is passing without looking. All these sea noises embody his longing for distant lands. Near the beginning, a boat whistle changes into the wheezing of the coffee maker in the bar, bringing together through sound the two jobs he is torn between, underscoring the hard choice he must make. Later, when Marius first accepts work on a ship, a sailor's song in the background about traveling around the world represents the fascination of such a life for Marius.

Sound is sometimes used to diffuse a tense situation. During a heated argument about Marius, when César has Panisse by the neck and

Panisse says, "I've knocked out bigger guys than you," a cork suddenly pops out of a bottle of champagne. The fight is forgotten as they taste the wine, deciding that it is not bad, but not properly chilled. At other times it is utilized to increase tension. Once, late at night, when Marius tells Fanny his decision to leave and they are trying to talk the situation out downstairs in the bar without waking César who is asleep on the second floor, a group of noisy revelers comes and pounds on the door. They finally leave, and Marius and Fanny make love for the first time.

However, it is dialogue that dominates the film, even though Korda and Pagnol cut a certain amount of expository material that was unavoidable in the theater. For example, there is no verbal introduction of Panisse. We only see him briefly sitting in a lounge chair at his sail shop, enough to let us know who he is and what he does.

Pagnol has said, "There must always be an underground current in a scene, which must contain everything that is not said."[13] The film's final scene illustrates this principle perfectly. César, who believes that Marius and Fanny are about to be married, gives Fanny his wife's room, which has remained empty since she died. Fanny, who is pregnant but who encouraged Marius to leave, realizing that she couldn't compete with the call of the sea, lets César go on, not telling him that his son has left. At the same time, the ship on which Marius has found work weighs anchor and heads out into the Mediterranean. Panisse calls from below, "Hoom! César, Marius is leaving!" But César thinks he is joking. It is here that César, who has been a study in comic irascibility throughout the film, drops his mask and lets his deeper feeling show through. It is not until Fanny faints that he realizes that Marius really is leaving. He leans out the window of the room, which would have represented to Marius a life of confinement and, as the ship under full sail heads out into the sun-filled waters, vainly calls his son's name. It is with this sequence that the second part of the Marseilles trilogy, *Fanny* (1932), opens.

When asked why his movies enjoyed such success abroad, Pagnol answered that he thought it was due to their authenticity. *Marius*, while exploiting the picturesque side of the old port, goes beyond the popular clichés about Marseilles to portray accurately the daily life of ordinary people there. The degree to which he succeeded may perhaps be measured by the fact that, although there have been several remakes of the Marseilles trilogy, none have been able to recapture the unique charm, despite some evident flaws, of the original.

Later Experiments in Sound

Le Grand jeu.   After making several distinguished silent films in France, Jacques Feyder surrendered to the siren call of Hollywood, where, for a few years, as he put it, he did no important work but learned

Pierre Richard-Willm and Marie Bell, first as the elegant, blond Florence, and then as the tawdry, dark-haired Irma in Jacques Feyder's Le Grand jeu. *Courtesy of Cinémathèque Française.*

a great deal. He returned to France in 1932 with an idea for a scenario derived from Pirandello's *As You Desire Me*. He had hoped to direct Greta Garbo in a movie version of the play but had been unable to sell the project in Hollywood. His plan had been to develop Pirandello's theme of the ambiguity of identity by replacing Garbo's voice during a portion of the film by dubbing in that of another actress.

Back in France, he adapted the idea to an entirely different story and setting, developing the scenario in collaboration with Charles Spaak. The result was *Le Grand jeu* (1933), the first of his films to be based on a narrative of his own conception. It relates the adventures of Pierre, a rich young Parisian, who embezzles funds to keep his extravagant and heartless mistress, Florence, in luxury. To avoid a scandal and to try to forget Florence, he joins the Foreign Legion. In Morocco, instead of oblivion, he encounters in a desert bistro a singer/prostitute, Irma, who uncannily resembles his former lover. Is Irma really Florence? Pierre never really knows, but he has almost suceeded in overcoming his doubts and is on the point of marrying Irma when, by chance, he meets Florence in the street in Casablanca. Although Pierre is still infatuated with Florence, she clearly cares nothing about him. Realizing at last that Florence is unworthy of his love and now unable to love Irma, he reenlists in the Legion and goes off to death on the field of battle.

The same actress, Marie Bell, plays both Florence and Irma, but the two characters are by no means identical. Florence's hair is an elegantly coiffeured blond; Irma's is a rather ragged dark brown. Florence's manner and gestures are refined and polished, while Irma's are slovenly. Nonetheless, the similarity between them is striking, and Pierre is stunned by it. The face, the eyes, the smile is the same. Can we have come upon his great love once again, fallen like himself from the world of limousines and lacquered furniture into the dusty depths of colonial society? The question torments him.

He desperately wants to believe that Irma actually is Florence, but it is the difference in their voices that holds him back. Florence speaks in lively, sophisticatedly brittle tones; Irma's accent is vulgar, her intonation stolid and weary. Only when Irma is silent can Pierre really believe that he is holding Florence in his arms once again. When they make love, he demands that Irma remain mute.

Irma is an enigmatic figure. Although he persistently questions her about her past, she cannot satisfy his curiosity. She has suffered a head wound and has partially lost her memory. She knows she has been in Bordeaux and Barcelona, but most of her life is a blank.

The dilemma completely disorients Pierre, filling him with doubts and hesitation. The dubbing device has the effect of drawing the spectator into his quandary, so that his uncertainty and apprehension is shared by the audience. Alexandre Arnoux, a film critic and script writer, describes the reaction of the public when the film first came out:

We were all struck by this displacement, by this disintegration of a character when stripped of her voice. It is physically unsupportable; unconsciously, we strive to put a broken individual back together again. Feyder, by making use of the very weakness of dubbing, obtained an astonishing effect. Thus the spectator participates in Pierre's anguish; thus the two heroines only merge and become identical silently. From the defects of a technical process, from a commercial trick, an artist has drawn a means of expression.[14]

Perhaps for the first time, Feyder uses sound to develop and penetrate the psychology of his main character. Had he stuck with his original choice for the role of Pierre, Charles Boyer, the impact would have been much greater, but Feyder and Boyer had a disagreement and the part went to Pierre-Richard Willm, an actor whose ability to communicate emotion was severely limited. With Boyer in the lead, the film might have retained today a great deal more of its initial power than it does. Nonetheless, its considerable success served to reestablish Feyder as an eminent director, allowing him to make, in quick succession, *Pension Mimosas* (1934) and his masterpiece *La Kermesse héroïque* (1935).

Le Roman d'un tricheur.   Sacha Guitry was primarily a man of the theater, an accomplished actor and the author of a vast number of successful boulevard comedies. His interest in the cinema coincided with the coming of the talkies. Like Pagnol, he saw at once the possibility of filming a play, which could then be shown in many different places at the same time, without having to bother with casting, rehearsals, sets, costumes, or any of the other mechanics of a theatrical performance. Although, unlike Pagnol, he never abandoned the theater, he made thirteen films during the 1930s, several of which enjoyed international success, and he continued to produce movies for the remainder of his life.

Although his first screen works were filmed theater, he quickly perceived a basic difference between the two media, predicting that "the cinema would have more to borrow from literature and from design than from the theater."[15] In keeping with this view, he made *Le Roman d'un tricheur* (1936), based not on a play but on a novel he had written, and in the film introduced an ingenious innovation in the use of sound.

The Story of a Cheat (as it was titled for its American release) tells the life story of a little boy who, because of a petty theft, is not allowed to eat some mushrooms his family has gathered. They prove to be poisonous, and his entire family of twelve dies. He concludes that he survived because he was a thief, while the others died because they were honest.

He becomes a pageboy, an elevator operator, and occasional gigolo and croupier at the casino at Monte Carlo. At the suggestion of a woman, he tries cheating and wins. From then on, he becomes a professional gambler and cheat, amassing a fortune, until he is convinced by an invalid who saved his life to go straight. As an honest gambler he gradually loses his wealth and ends up working for a playing card manufacturer.

The originality of the film lies in the way in which the story is narrated. It is told in the first person by the gambler, played by Guitry, who is seated at a table on the terrace of a café, writing his memoirs. There is almost no dialogue, yet the soundtrack becomes the essential element of the narration. The images on the screen develop out of the gambler's memories, but there is no strict correspondence between what is said and what is shown. Rather, the two elements are purposely disassociated. The gambler comments on and guides the flow of images which, in their own right, enlarge upon what he has said. This technique allowed Guitry to shoot the movie like a silent film, embellished by a witty voice-off narration, a procedure he continued to use, intermixed with dialogue, in his later movies.

Although Guitry did not follow up *Le Roman d'un tricheur* with any further audio experiments, the film paved the way for others who were later to become fascinated with innovative approaches to sound. It is possible to see the influence of Guitry's method in the opening presentation of the town, its people and customs, in Welles's *The Magnificent Ambersons* (1942). The British film *Kind Hearts and Coronets* (1949) is constructed around Guitry's narrative technique. And he may be considered a forerunner of Alain Resnais's separation of sound and image in *Hiroshima mon amour* (1959).

Truffaut has said that as a child he saw *Le Roman d'un tricheur* dozens of times and knew the soundtrack by heart. For him it represented a kind of blueprint on how to survive and make it as a completely self-reliant individual. As a director, he, too, has utilized voice-off narration extensively, in *Jules et Jim* (1961), *L'Enfant sauvage* (1969), and *L'Histoire d'Adèle H* (1976).

With *Le Roman d'un tricheur,* we come to the end of a rich period in the development of the vocabulary of sound in France. Although further refinements would be made, the basic territory of audio expression had been charted. The difficult transition from silence to sound was at an end. Other problems increasingly claimed the attention of both moviemaker and audience, not the least of which was the tangible movement of Europe, once again, toward war.

The many faces of Sacha Guitry in his Le Roman d'un tricheur *frame Jacqueline Delubac, the woman who inspires his career as a cheat. Below: Sacha Guitry, writer/narrator in* Le Roman d'un tricheur.

3

Empire and Exoticism

MARIUS'S longing for distant lands is a motif which has haunted the French psyche since the time of Baudelaire. Fleeing a routine, land-locked life, the waiter of the Bar de la Marine represents for the poet the purest kind of traveler: "But the true voyagers are those alone who leave / Just to leave . . . / And, without knowing why, always say: Let's go!"[1] Marius ships out aboard the *Malaisie* bound for the mysterious East by way of Athens and Port Said. By contrast, the hero of *Le Grand jeu*, like Baudelaire himself, is a reluctant journeyer, forced to depart from home at the behest of an indignant family council. Pierre is one of those wandering "Astrologers drowned in the eyes of a woman,"[2] and it is entirely logical that Blanche, the clairvoyant bistro owner who twice tells his fortune, also invokes the author of *Les Fleurs du mal* in the dusty wastes of the Sahara.

For those unable to travel, the cinema in the 1930s provided a means of escaping from their humdrum daily lives, and, judging by the large number of films with foreign settings, the demand for this type of evasion was considerable. Of the various locations, North Africa was by far the most popular. Although geographically close to France, it was culturally worlds apart, offering a background at once exotic and enig-matic. Here the myth of the voyage often joined with the dashing legend of the Foreign Legion, as in Josef von Sternberg's *Morocco* (1930). To a certain degree, the initial success of *Le Grand jeu*, which was refused Le Grand prix du cinéma français in 1933 only because it was judged immoral, can be attributed to the original way Feyder treated a subject already much in vogue. By the same token, if a good deal of the film's charm has paled today, it is because we no longer perceive the le-gionnaire as a romantic figure. The same is true of Duvivier's *La*

Bandera (1935), the film in which Jean Gabin began to emerge as one of the most charismatic actors of the decade.

Pépé le Moko

It was Gabin's performance in the title role of Duvivier's *Pépé le Moko* (1936) that firmly established him in the forefront of leading men. The film takes place not in the desert but in the Arab quarter of Algiers, where Pépé, a bandit tracked by the police, has taken refuge. There, protected from the police by the inhabitants, he has become a kind of boss of the Casbah. Although living with a native mistress, Inès, he falls in love with a French tourist, Gaby. When Gaby fails to appear at a rendezvous as promised, he leaves the Casbah to search for her. Inès, furiously jealous, alerts Slimane, the police inspector who has kept him under constant surveillance. Captured, Pépé commits suicide, as the boat bearing Gaby away slips out from the dock.

Pépé le Moko is basically a gangster picture which owes a good deal to earlier American examples of the genre, in particular Howard Hawk's *Scarface* (1932). But Duvivier does not simply imitate his models. He molds his raw material inventively, crafting a movie that is at once highly personal and unmistakably French.

One of Duvivier's main talents as a director was his ability to create atmosphere, and much of the film's impact comes from his evocation of the Casbah. It is a measure of his versatility that, in portraying the Arab quarter so effectively, he departed radically from his usual working methods. Having begun his movie career as assistant to André Antoine, the founder of the Théâtre-Libre, Duvivier retained a predilection for naturalism, especially for real-life rather that studio settings. For example, he went to great lengths to obtain an authentic background for *La Bandera*. Refused the assistance of the French Foreign Legion by the local commandant, a hard-nosed German who felt that his men were not in North Africa to make movies, Duvivier procured the cooperation of an obscure colonel in the Spanish Foreign Legion named Franco. Although Franco was most helpful, Duvivier still went through considerable hardship, setting up headquarters in Ceuta and riding hours each day by truck to reach an isolated desert location. His attention to detail was so scrupulous that certain parts of the film convey, with almost documentary accuracy, the daily life of a legionnaire at the time.

Given this realistic penchant, it is curious to note that the overwhelming majority of *Pépé le Moko* was shot in the studio, using sets created by Jacques Krauss, in preference to the actual Casbah which would no doubt have offered interesting photographic possibilities. The few exteriors of the area near the entrance to the Casbah and of the port were shot in Sète and Marseilles. Occasionally even painted backdrops, the ultimate in artificiality, are visible. Duvivier's direction combines with Krauss's imaginative decor to give a highly romanticized view of the quarter, accenting everything that is exotic and picturesque. The streets are narrow and tortuous, often teeming with humanity. The houses are clustered against one another along the crooked streets that climb the hill from the port. The uneven pavements seem to exude local color: the beggar intoning his plea for alms, the water carrier from behind whom Gaby suddenly emerges into Pépé's field of vision, the beat of the tam-tam, and arguments between small shopkeepers and merchants. The real exteriors often seem pallid, almost repellent by comparison.

What is missing from this glamorized version is the actual squalor of the Casbah, the poverty, disease, flies, and bad smells of primitive sanitary conditions. However, such sordid details would only detract from the zone's mythical nature. The cramped, sinister alleyways of the Casbah have never served as a safe house for foreign crooks. Its image in the film is a skillfully wrought fantasy, exemplified by a beautifully smoky shot of one of its crowded streets that captures the quarter's hazily chimeric essence.

Despite the Casbah's obvious charm, Pépé has grown restive there. Like Baudelaire, who never finished his voyage to Calcutta, Pépé is fed up with travel, and bored with his surroundings and with Inès. Most of all, he is homesick and longs to return to Paris. Several times near the beginning of the film we see him sitting alone on the wall of his rooftop terrace, gazing moodily over the network of housetops stretching down to the sea, a prisoner in his own sanctuary.

In this sense, the very labyrinth of serpentine streets and constricted houses that keeps him beyond the grasp of the law takes on a claustrophobic character that presses in on him. At the film's outset, the Casbah is presented by means of a rapid, jumpy, nervous montage which begins at a police station located outside the quarter. As a local law enforcement officer explains to a group of scandalized police officials from the mainland why it is impossible simply to storm the Casbah and arrest Pépé. the camera moves out of the room and, from a high angle, sweeps over the rooftops of the Casbah, which appears like an urban maze. As the officer continues his explanation voice-off, a series of shots of the Arab quarter flicks onto the screen, its streets, its shops, its bars, and its people, each so rapid that it is impossible to grasp fully any one of them. Together they blend into an image of a bewildering, inpenetrable, potentially dangerous stronghold. The montage ends as the policeman finishes his presentation and the camera returns to the office. Aside from its obvious expository function, this elliptical movement of the camera—out from the station; over, in and around the Casbah; then back to the station—has the effect of covering it like a net. Pépé may be safe inside but he is always being watched and need slip up only once to fall into the clutches of Slimane, who is waiting with the patience of a chess master to checkmate his quarry.

Duvivier accents the image of the Casbah as prison by several shots of iron grillwork. During the aborted raid on the quarter, we see the police running across a street through the bars covering a low window. Inès is also seen looking out through the bars of a different window. The motif of obstruction culminates in the locked gate of the high steel fence which at the end separates Pépé from Gaby. At the same time, it merges with that of the net, as Pépé, having fallen into Slimane's trap, helplessly watches the ship pull away, his desperate calling of her name drowned out by the boat's whistle.

Duvivier also introduces the theme of male comradeship, which runs through most of the films of the period set in North Africa. It is present in *Le Grand jeu* in the friendship between Pierre and his fellow legionnaire, Nicolas. Indeed, in their uncomplicated camaraderie, Pierre seems much closer to his soldier buddy than he ever is to Irma. Similarly, Pépé appears to be more attached and loyal to Pierrot, the young deserter whom he takes under his wing, than he is to Inès. One of the most powerful scenes in the movie occurs when an informer, Régis, played with appropriate oiliness by Charpin, tricks Pierrot into the clutches of the police. Members of Pépé's gang force Régis to play cards while they await word of Pierrot's fate. As the time passes, Régis grows more and more anxious, fidgeting and sweating profusely, his nerves further frayed by one of the gang who calmly plays the harmonica. Finally Pierrot, who has escaped, returns, mortally wounded. Supported by Pépé and another of the band, he confronts his betrayer, shooting him dead. As Régis falls, he knocks against a player piano, setting it in motion, and its wildly incongruous mechanical notes fill the air. The camera moves from Régis to the face of the hoodlum who is perpetually smiling and to the dapper Jimmy (Gaston Modot), who is amusing himself with a child's toy, a cup and ball on a string.

Duvivier also uses music to help establish the tension between where Pépé is and where he would like to be. Those portions of the score which evoke the Arab quarter were written by Mohammed Yguerbouchen, whose work on a previous short film about Algeria Duvivier admired. The shrill, discordant notes and the rhythms of the Near East are present from the opening montage onward, not only reinforcing the effectiveness of the decor but underlying Pépé's alienation from his surroundings as well. To express Pépé's longing for Paris, Duvivier utilizes the music of Vincent Scotto, an immensely popular composer of hit songs, operettas, and film scores, who occasionally appeared as an actor in Pagnol's films. His chansons, like the one Tania (Fréhel), now old and fat, sings again to accompany a scratched and beat-up phonograph record she had made in her youth, embody all the haunting nostalgia that Pépé feels for his lost homeland.

Gaby symbolizes Paris to Pépé, and their love inspires him to sing one of Scotto's songs from the rooftops, to the amazement of the local people accustomed to his habitually morose cast of mind (a scene for which Gabin's beginnings as a minor performer at the Folies Bergères and cabaret entertainer stand him in good stead). In another sequence a metro ticket inspires them to take an imaginary journey across Paris, he leaving from the suburbs, she from the Champs-Elysées, passing station after station until they meet at the Place Blanche. Their fatal passion is foreshadowed early in the film, when Duvivier first introduces Pépé. At the beginning of the scene, we hear him but see only his hands and his feet. In one hand, he holds a pearl. He also sketches in the layout of a bank. The pearl links Pépé visually to Gaby, who is always bedecked with jewels, the gift of the rich and unattractive man with whom she is traveling. She and Pépé share a common interest: precious stones and money.

Their romance gives expression to a myth closely allied to that of the voyage: salvation through love. Pépé, despite a highly checkered past, dreams of going away with Gaby and starting life anew. Twice he makes a desperate dash down streets toward the sea. On the first occasion he stops within the confines of the Casbah. On the second, his descent is more resolute. The camera travels with him, at times showing his determined face framed against a deliberately fuzzy background of the streets and houses he is passing. At other times the camera follows behind him, his body set against a vision of waves, the sea, and escape. But his dream of a new beginning is not to be and he dies, never sure whether Gaby really loved him.

The film was a great success both at home and abroad. It so impressed American movie executives that they invited Duvivier to Hollywood, where he made *The Great Waltz* (1938) (a description of which much later became a chapter in Manuel Puig's novel, *Betrayed by Rita Hayworth*). Duvivier was originally hired by MGM to do a remake of *Pépé le Moko*, a task from which he was fortunately spared. Two pallid American versions were made, however, *Algiers* (1938), starring Hedy Lamarr and Charles Boyer, who dreamed of playing screen heavies but was much too gentlemanly to fill Gabin's shoes, and *Casbah* (1948), in which Tony Martin carries Pépé's crooner tendencies to ludicrous extremes. Much more important was the considerable influence which *Pépé le Moko* exerted on later French films of the decade, in particular on Marcel Carné's *Quai des brumes* (1938) and *Le Jour se lève* (1939). In both works Gabin again plays a tough, street-wise but world-weary hero who hopes to find redemption through love and start a new life—in *Quai des brumes* by sailing away to South America. In each case, like Pépé's, these dreams are crushed and end in death. So often did he play out a similar scenario that violence, despair, death, rebirth in love, and a voyage to start life over all formed an intricate part of what came to be known as the myth of Gabin.

The Defense of Colonialism

Légions d'honneur.   In *Quai des brumes* Gabin plays a deserter from the French colonial army, and the film represents a distinct current of disaffection with the values of the establishment that developed during the second half of the decade. At the same time, a number of movies appeared that were frankly sympathetic to the military, particularly in its role of maintaining France's position as a major imperial power. Maurice Gleize's *Légions d'honneur* (1938) was one of these.

Légions d'honneur tells the story of two officers serving together in the Sahara who are wounded in a desert skirmish. Given leave to recuperate, they go to the home of the older officer, Captain Dabrau, in the south of France. Dabrau is strangely distant with his young wife and arranges that his friend, Lieutenant Vallin, keep steady company with her. The two fall in love, and Vallin decides to cut his visit short rather than betray his captain's confidence. But when Vallin is telling her his difficult decision, Dabrau comes back unexpectedly. He does not recognize Vallin, but wounds him in the hand as the lieutenant takes flight. To avoid betraying Mme Debrau, Vallin explains his wound to his superior officers by claiming he shot himself voluntarily, an inexcusable act of cowardice. Court-martialed and stripped of his rank, he immediately reenlists as a common soldier and dies on the battlefield, having demonstrated exemplary courage and proved himself unquestionably worthy of his legion of honor.

This somewhat banal plot is rendered more interesting by what for the time was an unusual narrative structure. The film opens with the sequence of the military trial, in which the austerity of language and setting is broken only by the very moving testimony that a general—under whom Vallin had served bravely—gives as a character witness. Then, the bulk of the story is told in a long flashback, a technique which, although it has since become commonplace, had been used only rarely in cinema up to that time. Before reporting for duty as a private, Vallin leaves a long letter with his lawyer to be delivered only in the event of his death, explaining the truth about his wounded hand. As the lawyer reads the letter, its contents become the subject matter of the flashback, and the mystery of the injured hand is gradually explained to the audience.

As in *Le Grand jeu* the theme of friendship among men is again prominent and set off against less satisfactory relationships with women. Gleize devotes a certain amount of time to depicting the daily life of the troops and the officers in the desert outpost in Southern Algeria and to the conversations between Debrau and Vallin as their close rapport is established. It is on one of these talks that the captain tells the lieutenant prophetically, "The bush country unites, women separate." As soon as they return to France, it becomes evident that Debrau cannot begin to relate to his wife in the same way that he does to the young officer. He seems to have everything there, a beautiful ranch and a lovely spouse but he confides to Vallin that, when he is home, he misses the desert. He spends every day working energetically in the fields. We see shots of him riding herd on the bulls he raises, edited so that the thrust of his vigorous efforts comes first from the left, then from the right of the screen, presumably to meet head-on, canceling each other out. At night, he falls asleep quickly in his armchair, exhausted from this strenuous activity. His wife, so happy at his return, soon grows restive. Apparently his assiduous cattle raising leaves him sapped of the zest required for the pleasures of the bedroom, a situation which lends a certain irony to his particular choice of livestock. But it is evident that he exhausts himself on purpose, to avoid having to meet the needs of a relationship with which he somehow cannot cope. His wife is left to her own devices in the idyllic surroundings of the farm, a kind of orphan in paradise. It is not surprising that she turns to Vallin, with whom she has much more in common, for the affection her husband denies her. But, in the end, it is the friendship between the two men which wins out. Although he loves Mme Debrau, Vallin will not betray the trust of his captain. Although she begs the lieutenant to take her away from her loveless Erewhon, he plans to leave alone.

This strong sense of honor is paralleled by a strict devotion to duty which causes both men to acquit themselves with forthrightness and courage on the field of battle. Their honorable conception of war contrasts sharply with that of the Arabs. The French squadron that Debrau and Vallin are leading across the desert falls into enemy ambush because they are betrayed by their native scouts, who signal them to advance directly into a trap. Such subterfuge is implicitly impossible on the part of the two exemplary French officers.

Yet neither man, so capable in military surroundings, is able to deal effectively with the exigencies of civilian life. Vallin confesses his near total innocence in the ways of the world. An orphan who attended Saint-Cyr, the French equivalent of West Point, and then went directly into the service, he seems almost as ill-equipped to handle his social and emotional problem as Debrau. Like those other misfits of society, Pierre in *Le Grand jeu* and the murderer hero of *La Bandera,* he can only redeem himself and reestablish his good name through valor and death in battle. He dies in every way a credit to the army to which he devoted his life and to the school from which he graduated.

Trois de Saint-Cyr.   If *Légions d'honneur* is by implication supportive of the French military effort in snuffing out resistance in the North African colonies, Jean-Paul Paulin's *Trois de Saint-Cyr* (1938) comes very close to straight propaganda. It is the story of three cadets at Saint-Cyr. Two are fresh recruits, the third a seasoned veteran of the academy. The latter, Mercier, perfectly embodies the virtues which the college seeks to instill: self-control, patience, devotion to duty, obedience, organization, and self-discipline. He carries the student rank of adjutant and is the advisor of one of the new arrivals, who soon come to admire him immensely, and the three become fast friends. One, Le Moyne, introduces Mercier to his sister, but their budding romance is hindered by the sudden financial difficulties of Mercier's mother, a widow who is swindled out of her inheritance. Mercier is obliged to borrow money to complete his training at Saint-Cyr, with only his honor as collateral. Under the circumstances, he feels unable to propose marriage and, after graduation, requests an assignment in Syria. In due course, his two younger friends join him. Le Moyne, whose sister has accompanied him to the Near East, dies a heroic death defending a pipeline outpost from an insurgent attack. His sister and Mercier finally agree to marry.

Here the military virtues implicit in *Légions d'honneur* become the subject matter of the film. The first part of *Trois de Saint-Cyr* was actually shot at the academy and marked the first time that the doors of that august institution, the day-to-day workings of which had hitherto been shrouded in mystery, were thrown open to the public. During three years of schooling, we see how an elite corps of officers, the backbone of the French army, is formed. The seemingly futile task of setting out a box of matchsticks in the courtyard in a row, in order to report back how many paving stones and centimeters will be covered, teaches absolute obedience, patience, and discipline. Scenes of everyday life in the dormitory, the mess hall, and the lecture hall show the development of an esprit de corps among the students. As one general puts it in a pronouncement worthy of General Haig, "Saint-Cyr is a large family, of which I am the father." The cadets earn the right to wear the red and white plumed shako reserved exclusively for Saint-Cyriens by keeping an all-night, armed vigil, underscoring the chivalric image of the military career taught there.

This concept reaches its apogee in the death of Le Moyne. Outnumbered, he is mortally wounded before his two friends are able to arrive with the reinforcements which rout the enemy. They find him near death at the last machine gun in the fort, draped symbolically in the fallen French flag. His nickname, from Saint-Cyr, "le bazard" (the hawker), is passed on to the officer who replaces him in charge of the garrison, demonstrating an unbroken chain of command. The sequence ends as a general, to the stirring notes of "La Marseillaise," exhorts fresh troops to "Be ready, like him, for the supreme sacrifice, if one day the grandeur of our France demands it!" "The hawker" was the son of one of the country's wealthiest bankers, but France does not hesitate to sacrifice even its most gilded youth on the sands of the desert.

Le Moyne's death parallels that of real-life heroes of the colonial wars like Henri de Bournazel, who died under fire in the Tafilalet during the conquest of Morocco. Films like *Légions d'honneur* and *Trois de Saint-Cyr* also provide a counterpart in the realm of fiction to the considerable prominence accorded to the military in both the press and newsreels during the 1930s. Both movies had the active assistance and participation of the armed forces and were highly successful at the box office. *Légions d'honneur* won the Grand prix du cinéma français and the Grand prix du cinéma nord-africain. And one enthusiastic journalist went so far as to suggest that *Trois de Saint-Cyr* be shown to the Germans, to give them second thoughts about taking the French army too lightly.

Such films clearly answered a need to shore up public confidence in national defense at a time when the clouds of war were once more hovering over Europe and France's position, ringed by fascist states, was becoming increasingly untenable. By focusing attention on the existence of an elite core of dedicated officers, they helped answer in the affirmative the question raised by the documentary *Sommes-nous défendus?* (1938). They also afforded spectators a means of escape from the stubborn economic, social, and political problems which beset mainland France to the colonies where things appeared to be going much more smoothly.

The Illustration of Colonialism

As the title of the film *La France est un empire* (1939) indicates, the French were proud of their empire, the second largest in the world. In 1931 the Exposition coloniale in Paris—which attracted four million visitors—celebrated the fourteenth of July with a spectacular parade of colonial troops. This dashing display was echoed in movies like *La Bandera*, which contains four separate marching sequences, and *Le*

Grand jeu, for which Feyder, having been shown the route in advance, shot the arrival of an actual detachment of legionnaires at the barracks in Sidi-Bel-Abbès in one take with three cameras strategically placed along the road.

Although there was considerable curiosity about French overseas territories, these areas in reality played a minor part in the daily life of the average citizen, who possessed little accurate knowledge of them. Only North Africa, in particular Algeria, attracted many French emigrants. French Equatorial Africa a huge expanse of land, never drew more than 5,000 settlers, most of whom were civil servants. Nor did films set in the empire, which dealt more with the myths than the realities of colonialism, provide an accurate picture of life there.

In these movies, French imperialism is never called into question. The French cause, implicitly just, gains further support from the idea that, as one officer in *Trois de Saint-Cyr* says, "Colonialization brings peace," and that French conquest will bestow civilization on previously barbarous lands. Cooperative natives like those who participate in the defense of the outpost in *Trois de Saint-Cyr* are considered reasonable. But those who oppose the French takeover of their countries are portrayed by implication as perverse and irrational beings, unprincipled and untrustworthy, like those who ambush Debrau and Vallin—or like the American Indian in the traditional Western, a genre with which the desert films share a number of elements: wide open spaces, cloudless skies, cavalcades through desolate country with the flag snapping in the wind, bugle calls, the desperate defense of hopeless positions, reinforcements which arrive in the nick of time or too late, and, most important, a Manichean mentality. The enemy are "salopards," scum to be exterminated with righteous indignation. Those inhabitants who remain neutral tend to be relegated to the function of providing local color. In *Le Grand jeu* the desert garrison town is presented by means of a brief and rapid montage, containing shots of crowded Arab streets; an Arab prostitute, seen in silhouette through a curtain; a short, devious-looking Arab man picking up an equally sleazy European whore, and a native belly dancer. Although this series of views sets the scene with great economy of means, it is also made up of a string of clichés: the crafty and deceitful Arab male, the lascivious brown-skinned female.

In the colonies French promises of progress were by no means always fulfilled; governmental and private investment was far from as extensive as it might have been:

Most of the old colonies survived like outmoded ghost towns from another era; the vast new ones slumbered on without much change, save for a gradual improvement in public health through the control of endemic and epidemic diseases. These vast underdeveloped areas provided only a meager market for

French goods and furnished little except foodstuffs in return. In 1929 only 15 percent of France's foreign trade was with the empire.[3]

Such a description brings to mind the seedy colonial backwater depicted in Jean-Jacques Annaud's *Blanc et noir en couleur* (1976). For most subjugated natives, the empire meant exploitation, cultural suppression—the missionaries in Annaud's film who burn a pile of African masks, similar to the one hanging on Marius's wall, as junk and are carried through the jungle by native bearers—and, at the worst, slavery. The hero of *Batouala*, a novel about Africa admired by Pagnol for its authenticity, says, "I will never tire of telling of the wickedness of the 'boundjous' [whites]. Until my last breath, I will reproach them for their cruelty, their duplicity, their greed."[4] The French preferred to govern through a small, Gallicized native elite, like the group of corrupt politicians in Ousmane Sembène's *Xala* (1975), one of whom refuses to speak Ouolof to his daughter, who, in turn, will not answer him in French. The rest of the population suffered from a policy of benign neglect which, according to Sembène, independence has done little to change.

In the 1930s cracks began to appear in the myth of beneficent imperialism. Early in the decade both Gide and Céline described deplorable practices and conditions in the Congo. In 1939, Camus reported on the crushing poverty of the people in Kabylie, a region of Algeria. And, although the cinema never came to grips with the dark side of colonialism, *Itto* (1934), by Marie Epstein and Jean Benoit-Lévy, made a sincere effort to give a more balanced view of the situation in Morocco, a territory only fully subjugated in 1933.

Itto

Based on the writings of Maurice Le Glay, an old Moroccan hand, the film is set in the Middle Atlas Mountains, where a steel-willed Berber chieftan, Hamou, has for several years successfully orchestrated tribal resistance against the French. His cause is undermined by the work of a French army doctor, Pierre Derriau, who wipes out an epidemic that is decimating the sheep herds of the Arabs and, later, the diptheria outbreak that is ravaging their children. Interwoven into the military conflict is a love story, a kind of Berber *Romeo and Juliet* involving Hamou's daughter, Itto, and Miloud, the son of one of Hamou's allies who renounces the war after Derriau cures his sheep. Although Hamou is implacable in his opposition to the marriage of the young lovers, they get together in spite of him and have a child. But Itto finally abandons both to die with her father as he makes a last solitary stand, deserted by even his own sons.

Itto stands apart from all the other films of North Africa in that it casts aside many of the genre's most cherished themes. No longer is the *beau légionnaire* at the heart of the action. The paradox of society's misfits and criminals becoming the purveyors of the very civilization that has rejected them gives way to a much more plausible scenario in which the doctor, bringing tangible benefits of progress, plays the most important part in winning the natives over. Marshal Lyautey, who organized and presided over Morocco as a French protectorate and was aware of the strategic value of physicians, said, "No fact is more solidly established than the role of the doctor as agent of penetration, attraction and pacification."[5] *Itto* depicts the process in far less calculating terms. Derriau has been working in the highlands for three years and has come to love the remote region and its inhabitants. His wife is much more attached to the amenities of civilization and urges him to accept a post in Rabat. He has almost decided to do so, when one day, making the rounds of villages, he comes upon a cluster of blind men. They have been waiting for him to pass for days, seemingly out in nowhere in a god-forsaken stretch of country, to beg him to cure their children, who suffer from the same disease that robbed them of their sight. Without his intervention, the young ones, too, will become sightless. Derriau goes to treat them and decides to remain in the mountains. It is interesting to note that the movie crew included a doctor who, like Derriau, traveled far and wide caring for local people who fell sick.

Even more significantly, *Itto* accords the Arabs the prominence and humanity they merit, portraying them with rare authenticity. In most films of the Sahara, the natives are conspicuous in their relative absence. Christian-Jaque's *Un de la légion* (1936) carries this trend to its absurd limit: not a single Arab appears on the screen. Duvivier tried to cast a Berber actress, Tela Tchai, in the feminine lead in *La Bandera,* but his producers insisted on the French actress Annabella (who later worked in Hollywood and married Tyrone Power), believing that she would draw better at the box office. They may have been right, but her performance as an Arab woman is, nonetheless, unconvincing. Certain films strayed so far from reality that they were not permitted to be shown in North Africa, lest their lack of accuracy cause resentment among the native population.

In *Itto* the racial balance is tipped in the other direction. The cast consists of about 50 French and about 800 Arabs. Even more remarkable, not one of the Berbers had any previous acting experience whatever. They are Chleuhs, wilderness tribal people, relatively untouched by civilization, but, in the estimation of Benoit-Lévy, "excellent natural actors."[6] Far from the dehumanized enemy of most desert pictures, they bring to the screen a natural grace and dignity, a strong sense of self

which Albert Camus describes in his short story, "La Femme adultère."
According to Marie Epstein, it was not difficult to elicit from them the
first-rate performances they provide: "There were many of them working together in their natural environment where they felt at home. They
were rather easy to direct."[7] In the film, they speak Berber, which is
translated into French subtitles, at the time an innovative technique
which contributed immensely to the naturalness of their behavior. Even
Simone Berriau, a singer at the Opéra-Comique with family ties to
Morocco, who plays Itto, does not speak French.

Itto marks the first time that the inevitable love motif in a desert
movie involves Arabs. The romance of Itto and Miloud, the leitmotiv
which unites all the action, is developed with great delicacy. Their first
night of love takes place on the evening of a war celebration of Hamou's
troops. In the confusion at the encampment, Itto slips away and joins
Miloud in a neighboring garden, the deserted tranquillity of which
contrasts with the crowded, frenetic activity of the camp, an antithe-
sis heightened in the editing, which cuts back and forth between the two
locations. The light which bathes the solitary tenderness of the two
lovers is extraordinarily pale, a mixture of fragile blue, white, and silver
which turns the garden into a magic place. They become lovers in the
shadow of the palm trees and are awakened by an exquisite sunrise
which the camera holds only briefly. This subtlety of tone, which is
echoed later, when the separated lovers find each other once again at a
watering place, lends to their affection a lyricism and sensitivity unusual
in films of war. Since Marie Epstein has said that this striking natural
illumination was simply there, waiting to be taken advantage of, it is
curious that other North African movies of the period exhibit such a
uniformly pallid, washed-out, monochromatic hue.

Unprecedented care is taken in *Itto* to present a picture of the
mountain people, their life style and mentality. Hamou's *souk*, or
nomadic marketplace, and an Arab wedding are depicted vividly. When
two tribal chiefs reach an agreement, we see them exchange hats to
cement the accord. We learn of the belief that a person who touches the
breast of a nursing mother becomes sacred, an indication of the rever-
ence for human life in that harsh land. Finally, an unsophisticated native
samples all of the doctor's medicines at once to make himself immune to
all illness. Needless to say, he finds immunity in death.

In another uncommon departure from the norm, Hamou's fight is
characterized as a noble cause, and the French respect him as a coura-
geous, skilled, and altogether formidable warrior. This image is in keeping with that of the real-life Hamou, who for many years successfully
resisted Marshal Lyautey's efforts to extend French hegemony into the
Moroccan hinterlands, and whom Lyautey referred to as "mon bel

ennemi."[8] Unlike the usual, reprehensible *salopard* who routinely stoops to such tactics as shooting the enemy in the back or poisoning and drying up wells, it is Hamou who takes a heroic final stand alone against a hoard of adversaries in a hopeless defense of his last remaining stronghold, preferring to die in battle rather than surrender his primitive liberty. He represents well "The independent spirit of the Berbers, the sense of honor, the intransigence and the violent refusal to submit to power, above all to that of the foreigners . . ."[9] who have been trying to conquer them since the thirteenth century B.C. When he and his daughter fall, slain by a French soldier disobeying strict orders not to fire, the French troops present arms to show their admiration for his valor as the two bodies are taken to his capital for burial.

The film sets up an opposition between the French and Arab worlds which is expressed by a kind of parallelism between them. Before combat, for example, the French troops sing the lighthearted folksong "Auprès de ma blonde," Hamou's forces a harsh-sounding war chant. Similarly, the military leaders of each camp give their battle strategy to their soldiers. This polarization is finally resolved symbolically through Itto's baby, and throughout the film a link is established between children and the armed conflict. When Hamou's city is threatened, he orders the evacuation of women and children. In a finely paced sequence, they stream out of the town, infants and baby lambs carried on camels. Later, a shot of a hand on a gun signifies death. An analagous view of a hand on stalks of wheat is joined with the birth of Itto's child, photographed strikingly in silhouette through the canvas of the tent that serves as a delivery room. Subsequently, when Itto sings the baby to sleep, the lullaby contains a line about war and we see several rapid cuts of men going off to battle. Similarly, Françoise, the doctor's wife, sings the same lullaby, "Fais dodo, l'enfant sage" (words by H. G. Clouzot), that is sung to a dying soldier. When the hostilities interrupt the delivery of diptheria vaccine to Darriau, whose own infant has fallen ill, it is Itto who laboriously drags the case of medicine to him through a blinding snowstorm (the storm also cut the film crew off from supplies and provisions for several days). Finally, before going off to join her father, Itto leaves her daughter outside the doctor's house. His wife finds her and, overcoming her antagonistic feelings toward the Berbers, nurses the baby with her own, an act which reconciles the two worlds in a way that war never could. (In real life, Itto's child grew up to become a producer for French television).

Benoit-Lévy believed that the cinema could be a powerful instrument of education and, while making *Itto*, he organized film showings for the Chleuhs, who had become his friends. He undertook *Itto* because, as he said,

In all parts of the world there are men whose daily life, although different from ours, is no less poignant. Africa and the Orient are not only lands of wild fantasies, of whimsical palaces, of conventional princesses and other junk from the bazar. There are also joy and suffering over there that are simple and true, accessible to everyone, and which are worthy of being related to our own, so that we can feel the close similarity.[10]

Although the film he made never comes to grips with the fundamental ethical problems of imperialism, is by no means free from the paternalistic attitudes of colonialism, and places excessive faith in the wonders of Western medicine, it nonetheless stands as a highly original effort which breaks new ground, a sincere attempt to present the truth rather than the myth of North Africa. Unfortunately, although it was one of the great box office successes of 1934, *Itto* did not signal a trend in this direction. For the remainder of the decade, directors preferred to return to the comfortable clichés and racism of earlier desert films. Not until well after World War II is it possible to find a film like Jean-Louis Bertucelli's *Ramparts of Clay* (1970), which treats the Saharan mountains and their people with such austere authenticity.

Pacifism

La Kermesse héroïque. In its attempt to replace guns with the benefits of modern science, *Itto* merges with a current of pacifism flowing through the international cinema of the period. During World War I, French intellectuals had been vociferous hawks, but the devastation that conflict wreaked on France, both physical and moral, turned the succeeding generation of the intelligentsia into firm haters of war. The surrealists were bitter in their condemnation of such hostilities, an attitude reflected in Clair's *Entracte*. On the political front, Aristide Briand, who often served as France's foreign minister and was an ardent supporter of the League of Nations, even went so far as to propose a united federation of European states in 1929. This desire to dissolve the frontiers between countries which so often lead to armed conflict finds fictional embodiment in Giraudoux's novel, *Siegfried et le Limousin*, published in 1925, and in Gance's *La Fin du monde*. The film relates, with Gance's baroque touch, the formation of a universal government on earth under the threat of a comet, which is headed on a collision course with the planet. Once the single nation is established, the comet fortuitously veers away.

At the outset of the 1930s, several foreign antiwar films made a strong impression in France, in particular Lewis Milestone's *All Quiet on the Western Front* (1930), from Erich Remarque's novel and G. W. Pabst's

Westfront 1918 (1930). His *Kameradschaft* (1931) also represents an effort to break down the barriers between France and Germany. Raymond Bernard's *Les Croix de bois* (1932) is a harsh condemnation of the horror and futility of war. Bernard, who saw combat briefly in World War I, assembled a cast in which only actual veterans were permitted to appear as soldiers. In addition, each actor was given the same job in the film that he had held in the army. The result remains so convincing that in 1962, when the movie was shown on television, one veteran of the trenches of World War I was so overwhelmed by the equation of his memories and the images on the screen that he committed suicide.

Jules Romain, whose vast novel, *Les Hommes de bonne volonté,* covers the period of World War I and takes a distinctly dovish stance, helped form the Association of Revolutionary Writers, a pacifist organization designed to oppose the right-wing drift toward fascism in France. Gide and Aragon were also members. Alain, in his *Propos,* continually warned of the danger of accepting war as inevitable. Gance made a second version of *J'accuse* (1937) which, although marred by an implausible love story covering the period between the two wars, ends with a truly extraordinary summoning from the grave of soldiers fallen in World War I, a kind of resurrection of the dead from all the combatting nations. Against the backdrop of a racing, stormy sky, the air smelling of sulphur, the slain warriors return, superimposed on tombs, on the gate of the cemetery at Verdun, and on the commemorative cannons. Skeletons appear at the wheel of planes and trucks, statues spring to life, disfigured faces, crippled bodies join in a vast, macabre parade which is so fearsomely grotesque that it stops the nation, mobilizing again for war, in its tracks. Inspired by this terrifying spectacle, a universal nation is formed, as in *La Fin du monde.*

Surely the most unusual film with pacifist leanings is Jacques Feyder's *La Kermesse héroïque* (1935). Generally considered Feyder's masterpiece, it is a kind of antiwar movie *malgré lui. Pension Mimosas* (1934), which Feyder made after *Le Grand jeu,* although quite successful, was a gloomy picture, and he wanted to do something in a lighter vein: "After *Pension Mimosas,* I wanted to amuse myself with a farce, with an uncontroversial and safe subject, far removed from the events of today. . . ."[11] He had worked up such a script ten years earlier with Charles Spaak, but had been unable to find a producer. The success of his two previous films having created a much more favorable climate, he had little difficulty finding one this time.

The plot is set in the small, peaceful town of Boom in Flanders in the early seventeenth century, at the time when the region formed a part of the Spanish empire. The city is thrown into panic by the news of an impending visit from a duke, the ambassador-general of Spain, and his

military escort. Memories of the fierce duke of Alba and the pillaging by
his army years ago make the town leaders cringe at the prospect. The
burghermaster decides to play dead. The women of Boom, led by his
wife, Cornelia, take the town's fate into their own hands, meeting the
duke and his men and entertaining them with an elaborate banquet. In
many cases, they also bestow upon the visiting soldiers the favor of their
beds. The tactic suceeds admirably. The Spanish, charmed by such a
warm welcome, leave the next day in peace, exempting the locale from
taxes for a year in gratitude.

No such episode occurred in history. The film is a fantasy, an escape
into time rather than space. One of the most striking features of this
flight into the past is the scrupulous authenticity of costumes and decor,
both of which draw heavily on the masterpieces of the great Flemish
painters, whose works were consulted. Certain ones by Breughel, Hals,
Memling, and Jordaens are actually reproduced as scenes in the film.
Jan Breughel appears as a character engaged in painting a group portrait
of the town leaders, and it is he who finally marries the burghermaster's
daughter. The people in Benda's costumes seem to have stepped out of a
Flemish canvas, and Lazare Meerson's re-creation of a sleepy little
Flemish town, its canal, its streets, and its shops captures all the rustic

*Françoise Rosay, Jean Murat and Louis Jouvet in Jacques
Feyder's* La Kermesse héroïque, *a film distinguished by rigorously authentic costumes and decor.*

charm of a Flemish landscape. In his search for accuracy, Feyder consulted artists, museum directors, and scholars "to popularize and spread throughout the world the prestigious art of the great painters of my country of birth."[12]

The movie, working in a farcical vein like de Broca's *King of Hearts* (1967), succeeds in turning upside down and ridiculing some of the most treasured clichés of the war mystique. The themes of male comradeship, loyalty, self-sacrifice, and stalwart courage, central to *Légions d'honneur* and *Trois de Saint-Cyr*, are effectively parodied in the outrageous conduct of the Boom's leaders. When the mercenary arrives to deliver the message of the duke's imminent visit, the butcher, a particularly pompous alderman, is too terrified to speak and must point to direct him to the town hall. When the messenger steps into the doorway of the building, shot from a low angle so that he looks especially menacing, like a swashbuckler, silence reigns again, as the other aldermen shake in their boots. Later, the baker and the fish merchant, both members of the town council, hide their weapons, one in his oven, the other under a pile of fish. The burghermaster fleetingly offers to sacrifice himself for the general good, "if there must be a victim . . . let it be me!"[13] but quickly withdraws the suggestion in favor of the ruse of feigning death. Much is made of the ferociousness of the Spanish, their sacking of Anvers, and of what they will do to the women of Boom, "Your women and your daughters . . . savagely forced . . . will know rape and defilement" (17). A rapid montage evokes the horrors of war in Boom—its women tortured and violated, a group of corpses strung from the limbs of a tree, silhouetted against the skyline of the town. Nonetheless, the men simply abandon their women to their fate. Even love cannot inspire courage in such all-out cowards.

The myth of the bloodthirsty, implacable, barbarous enemy is also punctured. The duke is the picture of refinement, a man no more interested in doing battle than the good burghers: "I detest war and soldiers bore me!"(25). Nor is his retinue made up of merciless brutes. All are well-behaved and, like the duke, have no need of forcing women to enjoy their sexual favors. When the detachment leaves in the morning, having made love not war, a bouquet of flowers picked in the fields adorns every pike and musket. The only use to which the duke puts his sword is to bid a courtly farewell to Cornelia, after their night of romance.

The presence of mercenaries in the duke's force undercuts the idea of fighting heroically for one's country. One Swiss soldier has fought for France against Austria and for Austria against France. The only thing that counts is money, a fact that is not lost upon Boom's greedy hotel-keeper, who, as he starts to rake in the profits, says, "there's nothing like the army . . . no matter what army to get business going . . . we must have armies!" (36). His avariciousness adds a further dimension to the felicitous choice of the town's name. Boom, which exists in Flanders to this day, can mean in French "a sudden rise in prosperity" or "a party." And, of course, it brings to mind the sounds of war.

The film has had a very strange career. Received coolly at first in Paris, it went on to win the Grand prix du cinéma français in 1936. It was a smash hit in Germany, and came to be considered in retrospect, after France fell to Germany in World War II, as an apology for collaboration with the enemy, a judgment not without irony, since Feyder and his wife, Françoise Rosay, who gives an excellent performance as Cornelia, had to flee to Switzerland during the occupation. Feyder was named best director at the Venice biennale, and the movie ran for many months in London to packed houses. The Flemish were less enthusiastic, Belgium having traditionally been inhospitable to invaders. There demonstrations, stink bombs, and mice let loose in the theater disrupted showings. In Hollywood it won two Oscars, one as the best foreign film of the year. It was recently voted a *César* as one of the ten best French films ever made.

Le Drame de Shanghaï.   Pacifism is also an important theme in G. W. Pabst's *Le Drame de Shanghaï* (1938). The film involves a struggle for power between the Black Serpent, an oriental secret society as devious and deadly as its name suggests, and Tcheng, the idealistic young leader of a political movement seeking to unite the Chinese people and improve their lot. With the help of one of its operatives, Kay Murphy, the sect attempts to assassinate Tcheng, but a French journalist, Franchon, foils the plan. Tcheng triumphs over the Black Serpent at the moment when hostilities break out between Japan and China.

The China portrayed in the film is, like Duvivier's Casbah and Feyder's Boom, a fantasy. As Franchon's bureau chief tells him, "There is no China. It's not a country, it's a land of dreams. It's a country that sleeps, dreaming that it exists, but it doesn't." He makes it sound like just the kind of place Marius set off to find. Yet, if Shanghai was one of his ports of call, it is easy to understand why he returned a disappointed and bitter man. The city is neither glamorous nor picturesque. Its society is fragmented and corrupt and the Black Serpent is the symbol of its corruption.

Tcheng gives an impassioned speech denouncing the rampant social injustice in Shanghai. Unemployment is so high that even coolies are out of work. Families are forced to sell their children to survive. Over and over like a refrain he repeats the line, "This scandal must cease!" His message is one of nationalism: the Chinese can only rely on themselves in their efforts to break their chains.

Those world powers, like France, England, and the United States, who have carved out lucrative trading concessions for themselves in Shanghai, must share with the Black Serpent responsibility for the continuation of these appalling conditions. In the film, two drunken sailors from abroad admire an alluring prostitute. One says to the other, "She must be expensive." But his friend knows better: "Oh, no! You give her two dollars and she'll give you back some change." The scene serves as an image of foreign exploitation in Shanghai.

Another sequence illustrates how little value is placed on human life in the city. A coolie, presumably out of work, bows deferentially and enters a shabby room. The light from neon signs which flash on and off comes in the window from the street. Several thugs offer the coolie one dollar in return for taking an injection, without explaining what the injection is. He accepts and takes the dollar. They administer the injection. He laughs, then drops the dollar and falls dead on the floor. The Black Serpent has just tested the efficacy of the poison with which they intend to kill Tcheng.

Given such a dishonorable setting, it is not surprising that the theme of the voyage and the desire to start a new life appears again in the film. Kay Murphy, a Russian exile, has been singing in a night club, L'Olympique, for seven years. She has also been working for the Black Serpent and she considers the whole period a nightmare. Her daughter, Vera, whom she has educated in a finishing school in Hong Kong, has just graduated and is on her way to Shanghai, knowing nothing of her mother's unsavory connections. Kay plans to leave with Vera for New York and, as she packs, she discards an old shawl as she hopes to cast away her old life. But her desire, like Pépé's, is not to be. She, too, has too checkered a past. Ivan, her superior in the Black Serpent, whom she thought dead, returns and forces her to take part in the plot to murder Tcheng. In the end, Vera discovers the truth about her mother, and Kay is knifed as she is swept along in the crush of people in the streets when the Japanese attack the city.

Tcheng survives to lead a peaceful uprising of the people against the powers represented by the Black Serpent, a march for which workers leave their jobs and in which women walk beside men. The crowd passes through the streets, swelling in size, winding across a circular bridge into the machine guns of the establishment. Lee Pang, head of the Black Serpent, watches from a balcony. One of the lead marchers is gunned down, but that is the only bloodshed. Tcheng's repeated plea to the soldiers, "Do not fire on your brothers!" is heeded. The soldiers cross over and join with the protesters. It is a victory of passive resistance, of faith over weapons, before which Lee Pang symbolically effaces himself behind an Oriental fan. Yet at the film's end, the future of reform is left in doubt. The Chinese must use their newfound solidarity to repel the

Japanese invaders, whose fighter planes fill the sky over Shanghai. Smoke and fire consume the city as war breaks out. French, English, and American ships evacuate refugees, taking Franchon and Vera to safety.

Another movie set on the China coast, Jean Delannoy's *Macao, l'enfer du jeu* (1939), bears so many resemblances to *Le Drame de Shanghaï* that it is useful to discuss the two together. Delannoy's film begins where Pabst's leaves off, opening on a bombed-out Chinese town whose survivors are being lined up and shot by enemy firing squads. Hubert Kraal, an arms merchant with a direct hand in this mayhem, rescues a French night club singer, Mireille, from summary execution and takes her on his ship to safety in the Portuguese colony of Macao. There heavy debts place him in the merciless hands of Yin Chai, a banker with major underworld holdings. His criminal activities come to light through the efforts of a French journalist, Pierre, to the horror of his daughter, Jasmine, who knew nothing of his illicit undertakings. Kraal suffers the inevitable fate of a merchant of death unable to meet his commitments. Yin Chai, mistakenly believing he has caused Jasmine to die, goes mad and destroys himself and his illegal empire.

In his speech to the people in *Le Drame de Shanghaï*, Tcheng declares that peace is the only time in which great social reform can be accomplished, and he warns against the nefarious influence of arms traffickers and war profiteers. Kraal in *Macao* is such a man. Played with considerable flair by Erich von Stroheim, he is a kind of black sheep von Rauffenstein, a fallen aristocrat, always impeccably dressed in a white captain's uniform, with genteel good manners and a completely disillusioned view of the world. His ship is manned by a slovenly, lecherous crew of social defectives, over whom he exercises tenuous control and who rise up in mutiny when he cannot pay them. Yet he is capable of the most exquisite courtliness toward Mireille—"the first man who has given without taking."

Kraal finds his counterpart in Ivan, the Black Serpent operative portrayed by Louis Jouvet with appropriate malificence. Ivan, too, is an aristocrat fallen on bad times. If anything, he is even more corrupt than Kraal, seemingly devoid of scruples. He looks at a photo taken of him fifteen years ago and then at his reflection in a mirror and laughs out loud in despair at the decay that has set in. When Kay, in a desperate attempt to be free of him, shoots him, he asks, "Why didn't you do that fifteen years ago?" The colonies of the East seem filled with such sinister adventurers, like the Russian roulette profiteer in *The Deer Hunter* (1979).

Such places are also characterized by hypocritically corrupt societies, for the two underworld leaders, Lee Pang and Yin Chai, both pass for pillars of the community, prosperous and elegant businessmen, one of whom contributes heavily to worthy charities. Yin Chai, always dressed in a crisp white suit, frequently smiles, seldom speaks. Lee Pang talks with feigned humility, referring to Tcheng as "illustrious" and "very powerful," adjectives which fit him better than his young adversary. Each possesses a luxurious private dwelling, peaceful, idyllic, aesthetically soothing, with quiet gardens where they can enjoy the fruits of their misdeeds sealed off from the rabble they exploit. Lee Pang listens to Tcheng's speech in the tranquillity of his garden, snipping a rose as he begins to plot Tcheng's demise, as delicate melodious oriental music plays softly in the background. Yin Chai's house is like a labyrinth of elegantly furnished rooms and gardens, as devious in its architecture as its owner in his business dealings. Both also have at their disposal a public establishment which serves as a locus for their unsavory night-time activities. For Lee Pang it is L'Olympique, the night club where Kay sings and the chorus line is made up of exiled Russian women with no alternative means of support, whose telephone number is available to any customer from Big Bill, the ex-convict who manages the cabaret. For Yin Chai it is the Eldorado, the gambling den, from whose crowded balconies bettors lower their wagers down to the gaming tables in baskets made of bone. Pierre wins a considerable stake there, only to be relieved of it in the street by Yin Chai's thugs.

Into this world of scoundrels appear two thoroughly innocent figures, Vera and Jasmine. Both are young and inexperienced, having just finished their education abroad, and remain completely unaware of any parental taint of crime. As they learn the truth, their veils of innocence are drawn aside and they become cruelly conscious of the world's iniquity.

In each case they are saved from total disillusionment through the assistance and love of a French reporter, who functions as a beacon of honor in an otherwise dissolute society. Franchon loses his job rather than go along with a false report, planted by the Black Serpent and which his bureau chief is only too ready to send off on the wire that Tcheng is planning a coup d'etat. And it is he who saves Tcheng's life by starting a brawl in L'Olympique, which is filled with belligerent United States seamen, by yelling, "American sailors are bastards!" He manages to guide Tcheng out of harm's way in the ensuing confusion. Similarly, it is Pierre who courageously unmasks Yin Chai's infamous side and rescues Jasmine from the debris of her father's shattered empire.

The ending of *Macao, l'enfer du jeu* is more final, more devastating than that of Pabst's film, but perhaps that is because in Macao the decadence is complete, beyond hope of reform. Kraal sails his ship to Lepers' Island, the hangout of the arms dealers, where he is blown up during a naval shelling of the place, a fitting means and location for his death. Yin Chai goes insane, sets the Eldorado on fire, throws his money in the air above the gaming tables and shoots at it, and then is consumed in his own inferno. The epitaph for this apocalyptic conclusion could be taken from Baudelaire's "Le Voyage": "Bitter knowledge, that which one draws from travel! / The world, monotonous and small, today, / Yesterday, tomorrow, always, shows us our own image: / An oasis of horror in a desert of ennui!"[14] Are the colonies in the end an exotic dream or a grotesque reflection of their possessor? Or both?

L'Espoir

André Malraux knew China intimately, having written two novels chronicling the struggle of its people to overthrow those who were oppressing them. One of them, *La Condition humaine*, which won the Prix Goncourt in 1933, even contains a character who bears a more than passing resemblance to Hubert Kraal: Baron Clappique is a fallen aristocrat beset by problems with money, a gun merchant and gambler.

In 1938, having participated in the Spanish Civil War and written a long novel based on his experiences, André Malraux undertook to write, produce, and direct a film on the campaign. It recounts, from the point of view of those struggling to preserve Spain's republican government, the fighting in the region of Sierra de Teruel (the original name of the work). Since Malraux drew only one episode from the novel, the attack on a Fascist-held airfield, the movie represents a fresh view of the combat, one which reflects the declining fortunes of the Republican cause. By the time the film was conceived, Franco, seconded by Hitler and Mussolini, was moving closer and closer to victory, while France, England, and the United States stood idly by. Malraux intended to use the movie as a propaganda instrument to convince these democratic nations to support actively the efforts of the Spanish government to put down Franco's rebellion. An excellent earlier documentary by Joris Ivens, *The Spanish Earth* (1937), narrated by Hemingway in English and Renoir in French, was felt to be too austere for this purpose. By the time Malraux's film was made, however, his initial goal had lost its meaning. The war was over and Franco ruled Spain.

Malraux had to overcome formidable obstacles in the making of the movie. He spoke little or no Spanish but fortunately had the assistance of Max Aub, a Catalan poet with many useful connections, as interpreter and all-around helper. He also readily admitted to having no technical experience in moviemaking: "I am not a technician, but I think I have a visual imagination."[15] He went to work with a miniscule budget of about $25,000, under conditions which were not promising. Toward the end of the war, little in the way of equipment and film stock was available in

Julio Pena (center with wings), a foreign volunteer, watches the skies anxiously with other Republican fighters in Malraux's L'Espoir.

Spain, and studios were limited in scope and in comparative disrepair. During air raids, which averaged two a day, all electrical current in Barcelona was cut, which not only interfered with filming but made developing of the negative there much too risky. It was transported, with considerable difficulty, to Paris for processing.

For the cast, Malraux hired the best professional actors available in Barcelona. For the squadron fighters he selected some young soldiers who had seen action in the Republican army. In this respect the film resembles *Les Croix de bois*, using combatants to reconstruct battle scenes they had lived through. While the nonprofessionals fitted comfortably into their roles, those with a theatrical background were obliged to develop an entirely different dramatic style. José Sempere, who plays Commandant Pena, had been a vaudeville star frequently cast in the unmilitary role of a cuckolded husband. José Lado had been a tenor who weighed in at over two hundred pounds, whom deprivation had reduced to a sparse shadow of his former self. As a lean, tough partisan peasant, he is so convincing that early critics took him to be a simple farmer playing himself. José Lado's performance improves greatly as the film progresses and is an indication of the effectiveness of Malraux's directing, which sought to eliminate all trace of stage mannerisms. Relations with the actors could be trying. If shooting was scheduled to begin at 9:00 A.M., many would arrive, in proper Spanish style, at noon and insist on eating before starting work.

The movie contains highly realistic scenes of street-fighting, for which Malraux had to employ primitive techniques to achieve special effects. To give the impression of Franco's troops firing machine guns at Republican guerrillas, he had marksmen shoot their rifles at a distance of only twenty centimeters, blasting the ridge of a wall. In another scene, a car careened downhill through the street smashing head-on into a cannon, knocking it out of commission. After considerable searching, Malraux turned up a good auto body with no motor and requested from the performers' union a stuntman who could steer the car to the cannon and jump free at the last minute. The man who arrived got behind the wheel but unexpectedly abandoned ship as the auto went around the first curve. It turned over and was too damaged to be used again. When Malraux demanded an explanation, the man replied haughtily that he was an acrobat, but did not know how to drive a car. Malraux had no choice but to scrounge up another vehicle and reshoot the scene with another, more versatile performer (on another occasion he asked the union for another stuntman and was sent a ventriloquist).

The film's most powerful sequence comes at the end, when the pilot of a plane, Pena, crashes on a mountaintop and is carried down, severely wounded, passed from hand to hand and followed by a procession of 2,500 villagers who accompany his slow descent, their dark-clothed bodies forming a black Z along the winding path against the stark, craggy slope. It is the only scene in the film with music, which is by Darius Milhaud. Drawn from an episode that Malraux had actually witnessed, it serves as an image of a wounded Spain on the brink of defeat.

Malraux left Barcelona and crossed into France just hours before General Mola captured the city, the last bastion of Republican resistance, having been able to shoot only one half of his original scenario. The central episode, calling for the use of tanks, had had to be discarded—none could be spared from the front. What remains is a fragmented narrative structure which, combined with Malraux's rapid, nervous, clipped style, gives the film a documentary feeling. *L'Espoir* marks the first time that combat scenes were shot from the interior of a bomber, then an innovative perspective which has since become commonplace. It yielded the unusual image of an ant caught inside the sight of a machine gun being fired. Since the animal has no hearing, it does not react to the noise, and is for Malraux a symbol of man's fate: to be trapped like an insect in a mechanism he cannot understand.

Back in Paris, Malraux rerecorded the entire soundtrack and filled in the narrative gaps as best he could, even inserting a chase sequence with a squadron of Japanese planes from the film archives. However, the French government, not wishing to offend Franco or any other fascist regimes, withheld the movie from release. During the occupation, the Germans commandeered and destroyed every copy of *L'Espoir* but one, which escaped confiscation only because it was in a can labeled "Drôle de drame," the title of a 1937 comedy by Marcel Carné. No one knows whether it was improperly stored by mistake or by design.

L'Espoir, finally released in 1944, bears an introduction by Maurice Schumann with this theme: "Each face and each image, each look and each shot fired, everything tells us: the drama of Spain, it was already our drama; the war of Spain, it was already our war; and these men that we are going to see die were already dying for us."[16] War was no longer comfortably distant, a chance for society's misfits to atone with courage and death for misspent lives and for gallant officers to prove their mettle under fire on desert sands. War had come home from the colonies and Hitler, using tactics and forces he had tested with Spanish blood, blasted through the Low Countries, skirted the touted Maginot Line, and seized control of France with minimal opposition.

4

The Cinematic Mirror: Film and Society

"FRENCH SOCIETY of the 1930s is a sick society, physically weakened and morally traumatized by a world war of four years, still all too near. It is a society which remains bourgeois and rural, fearful and at the same time convinced of its superiority (intellectual or military). It is a society in crisis which moves forward masked. But by its masks, it wishes to deceive itself."[1] France was not only haunted by the specter of World War I but by the ever-increasing likelihood of World War II as well. One of the teachers in Christian-Jaque's *Les Disparus de Saint-Agil* (1938) repeats nervously, inanely, that "War is going to break out!" In answer to this threat, the country assumed a decidedly defensive stance, symbolized by the construction of the Maginot Line, begun in 1929. During the entire decade, the nation seemed gripped by a collective paralysis of the will, signaled by its timid response to Hitler's remilitarization of the Rhineland and to the Spanish Civil War.

Similarly, on the economic front, France tried to seal itself off from the ill-effects of the Great Depression by erecting a wall of protectionalism, adopting measures such as import tariffs and quotas. Needless to say, it did not remain immune from the financial crisis, which came later but lingered longer than in any other industrialized nation. By 1933, "The columns of the daily press were full of bankruptcies, scandals, and the suicides of businessmen and international financiers."[2] One of the most spectacular victims of the economic slowdown was the automaker, André Citroën. An aggressive, flamboyant entrepreneur, who brought the streamlined American manufacturing techniques he had learned working on the assembly line in Detroit to the Continent, he engaged in brashly un-European advertising methods like skywriting and placing neon signs on the Eiffel Tower. Characteristically, when the hard times struck, he elected to expand rather than retrench, retooling his plants to

Orane Demazis (Arsule) and Fernandel (Gédémus) are startled by noises in the underbrush around their campsite in Pagnol's
Regain.

make a new, front-wheel drive model. But panicky creditors, stepping in before production could get off the ground, reduced the "king of Paris" to insolvency, and he died soon after from that bane of the overextended, go-go businessman, bleeding ulcers.

Several equally stunning collapses rocked the film industry. Léon Gaumont and Charles Pathé, two pioneers whose names had become synonymous with French movie production, each saw their companies go bankrupt. While Gaumont-Franco-Film-Aubert's problems were a symptom of difficult financial times, Pathé-Cinéma was ruined by the mismanagement and outright thievery of its director, Bernard Natan (the discontented producer of *La Petite Lise*). Although neither firm actually went out of business, their production activity during the second half of the decade was drastically reduced and the shock caused by the discovery of their straitened circumstances was resounding. Depression–red ink also forced Paramount to bring its extensive output of original films at Joinville to an abrupt halt, and Tobis also cut back substantially filmmaking in its studios at Epinay.

Given such an unfavorable economic climate, it is hardly surprising that motion pictures, particularly in the first half of the decade, seldom came to grips with the problems which beset French society. As the cases of *L'Âge d'or* and Jean Vigo's *Zéro de conduite* (1933) quickly established, any attempt to criticize social rigidity and repressiveness risked swift and total censorship. Yet, if the cinema was not in a position to strip away the masks of society, it was able to make an accurate record of the manner in which society chose to be presented and increasingly, as the period drew to a close, to provide a glimpse at what lay concealed behind the facade of bourgeois respectability.

Both in its forms and in its content, the 1930s cinema reflects the image of an unbendingly reactionary social framework. We have seen how the French responded irresolutely to the coming of sound production, lagging far behind their competition in converting studio and theater facilities to accommodate the new technology. They also gave preference to those old and trusted genres, the boulevard farce and the melodrama, which hearkened back to the nineteenth century and were more suitable for portraying the *belle époque* than contemporary realities, affording the new patrons of the movies the comfortably predictable, reassuring, and unchallenging fare they were used to in the theater. Yet the elegant world of the idle rich portrayed in *Mon gosse de père, Ma cousine de Varsovie,* and many other similar films had, by the 1930s, become an anachronism, a throwback to earlier, more affluent times. Its persistence on the screen indicates how deeply embedded the resistance to change was in the social fabric.

Le Roi

Throughout the decade, following the success of *Ma cousine de Varsovie*, the team of Elvire Popesco and Louis Verneuil contributed numerous film adaptations of light theatrical confections, like *Le Roi* (1936). Directed with little imagination by Pierre Colombier, the movie revolves around the visit to Paris of the king of an imaginary foreign country. The royal guest prefers the unaffected charms of Marthe Bourdier, the wife of the wealthy industrialist at whose home he is staying, to the more pretentious and stuffy types with whom he is officially obliged to keep company. The two end up in bed together, but a contract which the king signs the next day, very advantageous both for France and for Monsieur Bourdier, lays to rest any ill-feelings. Although presented in 1930s garb, the play, which was a big hit at the Théâtre des Variétés in 1908, clearly shows its advanced age. Moments of cinematic interest, such as the king's arrival—with clips of actual parade footage followed by a studio shot of the monarch seated in an open car moving past a blurred backdrop of a crowd of well wishers, all timed to the snappy rhythms of the music which announces his appearance throughout the film—are few and far between. The considerable talents of Raimu are lost in the vapid role of the cuckold who places national and business interests before personal concerns. Although Gaby Morlay brings considerable zest to the role of Marthe, it is Victor Francen who saves the picture from utter staleness by playing the king with a finely modulated blend of good-humor and maliciousness. Francen went to Hollywood during World War II, where he acted in Duvivier's *Tales of Manhattan* (1942) and had a long, if not overly distinguished career, never finding a role there that took the measure of his talents.

Not only does *Le Roi* look back to a vanished era, it also contains a highly conservative message within its comic vicissitudes. Most of the action turns on the notion that, beneath all the pomp and circumstance, kings are just ordinary folk who, like their more modest male counterparts, sometimes want to sleep with other men's wives. But, since kings also wield great power, husbands should be indulgent when faced with the consummation of such royal desires. Regal largesse can go far in assuaging the sting of public embarrassment, and deference will pay off handsomely in the end. The film portrays a stiffly hierarchical society in which those of high rank enjoy certain privileges over those of lesser station, in this case distantly echoing the right of the medieval lord to sleep with the bride of any of his subjects on the wedding night. Bourdier's threats to seek satisfaction contain far more form than substance and when the marquis de Chamarande, on behalf of the government, makes clear to him where his interests and those of the nation lie, he quickly falls into line. In such a rigid social structure, it is neither seemly nor advantageous to protest too much.

L'Homme du jour

In Duvivier's *L'Homme du jour* (1936), the idea of a well-established social order in which everyone should keep his or her place becomes explicit. In the film, an unpretentious electrician, André Boulard, who dreams of being a music hall singer, achieves sudden notoriety when, by donating blood, he saves the life of a famous actress, Mona Thalia. Her plans to cast him in the role of protégé/lover never develop and, after a brief glimpse of life among the rich and famous, he is obliged to return to his former humble existence.

It is Boulard's lack of sophistication and basic decency which prevent him from capitalizing on his big chance. Although he lives and works in Paris, at heart he remains a hayseed from the country, and it is his very guilelessness that Mona at first finds attractive in him. A classical actress, she exclaims on first seeing her savior, "How simple he is! How handsome he is! An Alexandrin!" Thinking she means he's from Egypt, he corrects her by giving the name of the hick town he's from. Completely out of place among the elegant, he wipes his shoes on window curtains when they are "crottés," a word suggesting the animal dung of the barnyard. He gets drunk at the elegant dinner she arranges for him, addresses chic women as "my apple," sticks a copy of the newspaper with his picture on the front page in the outside pocket of his tuxedo jacket, and refers to Molière as "an ace."

Mona is, on the other hand, totally at home in her world, the luxuriousness of which contrasts sharply with the drab settings of Boulard's ordinary life. He discovers his sudden fame while riding on the metro, when the passengers recognize him from his picture in the newspaper. Then we see Mona in bed in the hospital, wearing an expensive robe, surrounded by flowers from her admirers, stroking an Angora cat. Later at the dinner party, there is an extraordinary moment when, to the accompaniment of a march, a table, which is also a fountain, rises from the floor inside the circle of guests. Through this opulent, astonishing, yet fatuous decor, Jacques Krauss (who did the sets for *Pépé le Moko*) is able to capture the affluent decadence of the upper stratum of society.

Mona takes André to her equally impressive country estate for a night of love which will, as she puts it, make history. But while she awaits him impatiently in her elegantly appointed bedroom with black velvet walls, dressed in white satin, he falls asleep in his own bed at the urging of his mother. Mona is so furious at being stood up that she throws a book at her cat and sends mother and son home in a separate car with the daughter of her cook.

Back in Paris, André finds that he has been replaced in the public eye by another phenomenon, a foreign acrobat who walks on his hands. He loses his job, his girl friend Suzanne dumps him, and his reward money is stolen. He goes to see Mona only to find her in the arms of another man, and he is reduced to trying to interest café patrons in his faded fame.

The film, an uneasy blend of musical comedy and satire, is not without faults, as Duvivier was quick to admit. The relative weakness of the work is perhaps surprising since Maurice Chevalier and Elvire Popesco were type cast in the lead roles and virtually play themselves. Moreover, the story bears a certain resemblance to Chevalier's own successful rise from humble beginnings. In fact, his recent experience in Hollywood had proved to be not unlike Boulard's. Spirited away to America in 1928 by Jesse Lasky, a Paramount executive, he was the darling of the American public in the early 1930s, starring notably in the comedies of Ernst Lubitsch. Then, suddenly, moviegoers there grew tired of him and he returned to France.

These similarities to Chevalier's own career lend a certain irony to the film's end, in which Boulard goes to meet Maurice Chevalier in his dressing room. Boulard asks whether the star thinks he has the right kind of face for the stage. Although they look exactly alike, Chevalier says no and goes on to explain to him rather pompously that the success of society depends on everyone remaining in his or her assigned role: "The place of an electrician is not in front of the projector." Boulard does not protest. The immobility of the social set-up could not be spelled out more didactically. Thus the transfusion which saves Mona's life has no lasting impact. André gives his blood without expectation of reward but Mona, who owes her life to him, ends by acting as if she owes him nothing, her earlier efforts to aid him motivated more by self-interest than gratitude. The mingling of their bloods becomes a symbol not of the breakdown of social barriers but of the vampirelike relationship of the rich and famous toward those of humbler state on whom their lavish lives depend.

The inflexibility of society is reflected also in the film's narrative structure, which is circular rather than linear, the hero returning at the end to his point of departure. The same pattern can be seen in numerous other movies of the period. The disillusioned anarchist of L'Herbier's *Le Bonheur* (1935), the sewer worker who serves briefly but brilliantly as head of state before returning again to his subterranean conduits in Christian-Jaque's *Le Père Lampion* (1934), and the industrialist whose career resembles Andre Citroën's in Jacques Natanson's *La Fusée* (1933) are only a few of many possible examples. The circular progress of their fortunes finds another real-life parallel in the famous case of Madame Hanau, herself a victim of the rigid society of the epoch. A financial genius of modest origins who ran a bank out of her head, without keeping any records, with dazzling success, she offered her customers 8 percent interest while all her competitors could do no better than 3. Her clients were the little people from all over France, schoolteachers, clergymen, retired military officers, and small shopkeepers, and hers was the only bank open at night so that workers could use it. But her liberal, populist banking ideas were her undoing; pressured by big business, the government brought her to trial, kept her in jail, and, in the end, ruined her. She finally committed suicide in her cell.

Mayerling

As Anatole Litvak's *Mayerling* (1936) illustrates, that traditional bastion of social inflexibility, the aristocracy, could also treat its own errant members with equal harshness. Based on a real-life love story, it recounts the ill-starred affair of Archduke Rodolphe of Austria and Maria Vetsara, the daughter of a provincial noble. Unfortunately, Rodolphe is already ensnared in a loveless union, a marriage of state, and any attempt to break free is met by his emperor father with unflinching refusal. The lovers' frustration finds its final expression in joint suicide.

Like André Boulard, Rodolphe is basically a passive hero, a type encountered frequently in the 1930s cinema. A sensitive man with distinctly liberal leanings, he cannot break free from the frozen formalism of the court. Accorded a great outward show of respect, he is essentially powerless. Courtiers bow and scrape before him, but he cannot even manage to obtain a consultation with his father when he urgently needs one. His frustration manifests itself in his moodiness and boredom, as in the brothel on his wedding anniversary, or in violence turned inward, as when he shoots his reflection in the mirror. In the end, he is without independence, like the marionettes in the park on the day he first meets with Maria. His passivism is set off by her contrasting animation—Danielle Darrieux went after the role aggressively and much of this energy spills over into her performance. But Maria is so dazzled at the idea of being loved by a prince that, although she is strong enough not to bow to the archduchess at a court ceremony when everyone else does, she, too, becomes totally submissive within the bounds of the relationship. Once she has taken the bold step of giving herself completely to Rodolphe, all her options have been exercised. Her life and her death are in his hands.

Had Rodolphe been content to take Maria as a mistress, suicide would have been unnecessary. But he wanted to make a clean break with the past, to end his marriage and start a new life, an unacceptable desire in such an immobile society which he can do no more to change than the students who riot on his wedding day. Rodolphe is the royal counterpart of the criminal outsider, seemingly defeated and doomed from the outset, like the string of heroes whom Gabin embodied in *Pépé le Moko, Quai des brumes,* and *Le Jour se lève.* He is just as trapped in the Viennese court as Pépé in the Casbah. In *Mayerling,* as in *Le Bonheur,* Charles Boyer's subtle performance makes an important contribution to the myth of failure, which became more pronounced as the decade advanced, repeatedly illustrating the futility of trying to carve out a personal destiny within a repressive social framework, a cinematic reflection of the breakdown of national resolve which culminated in the Munich accords.

Because a large pool of talented actors was readily available, most films of the 1930s, particularly love stories, lean heavily on strong secondary characters to sustain narrative interest. It is hard to imagine Pagnol's *Regain* (1937) without Fernandel in the role which established him as an actor of serious as well as comic dimension. And in Jean Vigo's *L'Atalante* (1934), Michel Simon's Père Jules, a part which he invented as well as portrayed, is perhaps the most convincing example of the pivotal importance of supporting players. Against this background, *Mayerling* stands apart in that, although its plot is quite simple, it has no noteworthy secondary roles. The only characters to receive significant development and focus are Rodolphe and Maria. Nor is their romance used as a device to link diverse elements of the film's action, as in *Le Million* or numerous colonial sagas. At a time when it was generally assumed that a couple could not by itself successfully maintain the dramatic tension of a feature film, *Mayerling* distinguishes itself as a tour de force in which the love story *is* the entire narrative, an achievement unduplicated until Bo Widerberg's *Elvira Madigan* (1967).

Just as the music of Mozart and exquisite photography play an important role in Widerberg's film, Litvak has given *Mayerling* a sumptuous *mise-en-scène,* creating an almost operatic atmosphere. The sets and costumes are lavish when portraying the opulence of the court, austere and imposing when projecting the power of the crown. The soundtrack contains music by Weber, Johann Strauss, Tchaikovsky, Honegger, and Jaubert. Waltz melodies provide an aural backdrop for the conversation in the park when Rodolphe and Marie first become acquainted. Later, Litvak expresses the flowering of their passion through the lushly romantic music of *Swan Lake,* superimposing shots of the park where they had their first rendezvous—the swans, the café, and the marionettes—over the actual ballet sequences.

The film made international stars of its leading players, providing long Hollywood careers for both Boyer and Litvak. It is perhaps fitting that

Boyer's final role was an excellent performance as another aristocrat, Baron Raoul, in Alain Resnais's *Stavisky* (1974), a film about the most famous con man of the 1930s. Litvak, who worked with Boyer again in several pictures, had the mischance to direct a most unfortunate remake of *Le Jour se lève* starring Henry Fonda and Vincent Price, *The Long Night* (1947). His most adventuresome American film was *The Snake Pit* (1949), a serious study of mental illness.

L'Etrange M. Victor

A society which prefers to remain masked must also remain a hypocritical one. In this connection, it is interesting to note the unusually high degree in which the theme of doubling appears in 1930s films. Sometimes it is confined to a brief sequence, as is *L'Homme du jour;* at other times it forms the very backbone of the narrative structure, as is *Le Grand jeu*. Quite often, it is linked to hypocrisy, subterfuge, and actual criminality. In *Abus de confiance* (1937), Henri Decoin cast his wife, Danielle Darrieux, as a young, impoverished law student who assumes the identity of the illegitimate child of a famous writer in order to dramatically improve her financial condition. The writer's wife eventually discovers the deception but prefers to let the ruse continue to spare her husband the cruel disappointment of the truth. In *La Chienne*, Lulu passes herself off as an American painter and, although she obviously has not a clue about her new profession, is lionized by the vapid art world. In Renoir's *Le Crime de Monsieur Lange* (1935), the publisher Batala, an exploiter of women, workers, and creditors, takes over the identity of a dead priest when things get too hot, because a man in a cassock can go anywhere and never be questioned by anyone.

In *L'Etrange M. Victor* (1937) by Grémillon, the twin themes of doubling and hypocrisy are at the core of the narrative. Set in the Mediterranean port of Toulon, the film tells the story of a man, M. Victor (Raimu), who leads a double life, at once a respected businessman and a killer who allows a poor cobbler, Bastien, to go to jail in his place. When after seven years, Bastien escapes, Victor hides him in his home, where the truth inevitably comes out.

Victor is a study in social duplicity. A successful merchant, owner of a large emporium, he is one of the prominent citizens of Toulon, well-known and highly regarded. To the outside world, he presents a good-humored, slightly absent-minded, rather indulgent facade. At the beginning, when his first child is born, he seems to be nothing more than a typically nervous, distracted, but proud father. Yet beneath this affable, nonthreatening mask, unsuspected by anyone, even his wife, lurks a receiver of stolen goods, a man as tough as steel. When one of his thieves tries to blackmail him, threatening to expose his chicanery, Victor does not shrink from silencing him forever. Then, although he testifies on Bastien's behalf, he allows him to be convicted. Years later, when Bastien escapes, Victor offers him enough money to flee to Switzerland and set himself up in business. When Bastien elects to remain in Toulon, Victor insists that Bastien stay in his house, where he lavishes favor on him. So attentive is Victor to the needs of his guest that his wife, Madeleine, is bewildered by his unusual largesse. But when at last he is cornered, his secret viciousness breaks out into the open again and he tries to strangle one of his accusers just before being taken into custody.

In addition to depicting the character of Victor, Grémillon paints an almost documentary portrait of Toulon. Interestingly, the city, like the protagonist, presents a double image. During the day, which is when we most often see it, its streets are almost always bathed in Mediterranean sunlight, full of bustling activity, women working, sailors strolling, and children playing. Even the narrow, cobblestoned, slightly sordid lanes of the old port are picturesque, like the heavily laden old boats that cross the harbor. The shops and the terraces of the bistros seem to exude an essence of *pastis,* garlic, and bouillabaisse. The entire city appears to be filled with music like the song which serves as a background when we

Jean Grémillon in L'Etrange M. Victor, *gives a taste of the local color of the "vieux port" of Toulon, the domestic squabble between Viviane Romance (Adrienne) and Pierre Blanchar (Bastien) Courtesy of Cinémathèque Française.*

first see the streets and the melody which Bastien, escaped from prison, listens to on the hill overlooking Toulon before descending into the town.

At night, however, it offers a quite different aspect. Darkness and disturbing shadows replace the radiant luminosity of daylight. The streets become peopled with prostitutes, drunks, and sailors looking for whores. Grémillon takes us into the cramped quarters of Bastien and his wife, where the couple is having a domestic squabble. Bastien listens in silent fury as she berates him until, fed up, he throws his dinner plate against the sink, goes out, and gets drunk, setting the stage for his false conviction. The warships which glide over the water in the harbor, some lit only by a few lanterns, seem more threatening after dark. The night music also turns ominous, like the sinister, rhythmic notes that issue from a café as Bastien walks by. Victor's crime is committed at night on an oppressively empty street, where he chokes his would-be blackmailer to death, after a whispered quarrel. As he makes his escape, shaken by his act, Victor leans for support against a wall on which his silhouette casts an enormous shadow, a graphic image of his two selves. Behind him is a notice warning against leaving trash on the street, an ironic reminder that he has just deposited a dead body.

Like Victor, the city is also capable of sudden, violent changes of aspect, such as the drenching rainstorm that abruptly engulfs it when Bastien returns. The downpour transforms its alleyways into streams and fortuitously shields the escapee's arrival from view. Such storms are typical of the region, and the sequence illustrates how carefully Grémillon, using a spare, unadorned style, integrated a portrait of Toulon into the film's narrative and thematic structure.

With *L'Etrange M. Victor* and *Gueule d'amour* (1937), two films made in Germany, Grémillon began once again to hit his stride as a director, following a barren period of work in Spain. Interestingly enough, Raimu later made another movie, Decoin's *Le Bienfaiteur* (1942), also built around the theme of a double life.

Avec le sourire

In such a rigid and hypocritical society, for maximum upward mobility dishonesty is surely the best policy. Maurice Tourneur's *Avec le sourire* (1936) recounts a success story in which this cynical attitude is the key ingredient. Written by Louis Verneuil and starring Maurice Chevalier, the film traces the meteoric rise of Victor Larnois, an illiterate but ambitious young man from the provinces, from theater doorman to director of the Paris Opera. Like *Le Roman d'un tricheur* it is a kind of scoundrel's progress.

Victor combines an aggressive, enterprising nature with a complete lack of scruples. He begins his career cutting dogs' leashes so that he can return the pets to their owners and collect a reward. When it comes to getting people fired whose job he covets, Victor is eminently resourceful, whether it be a doorman who has been rude to him or the theater director's assistant who plans to seduce his girl friend, Gisèle. But by no means all of Victor's gains are ill-gotten. He has a genuine flair for making money, devising a scheme of selling programs with stars' autographs which move like hot cakes. And he has the knack of turning a potential disaster into a bonanza. When the theater's banker commits suicide by jumping out of a plane over the English Channel, it looks as if people might assume that the theater as well as the banker is in trouble financially. Box office receipts could suffer, but Victor turns the story from a financial scandal (a reference to the actual death of a ruined financier named Lowenstein, who killed himself in the same way) into a tragedy of unrequited love. He creates the rumor that the banker was desperately in love with Gisèle, and not only does the theater escape any loss of revenue but the notoriety Gisèle gains transforms her from a mediocre, unknown singer into a star.

Victor's trademark is his broad smile, which we see often in close-up. It is at its most engaging when he is at his most ruthless. When the position of director of the Opera opens up, he bypasses all the would-be candidates languishing in the waiting room and blackmails the man who will decide who gets the job, producing a compromising document on his wife's past. Victor burns the damaging paper and the man assures him that he has the position. Then Victor, flashing his charming smile, informs the man that he has only burned a copy and that he will destroy the real record tomorrow, after he reads about his appointment in the newspaper.

Victor and Gisèle marry and she uses some of Victor's low-down tactics to break up the partnership at the theater between Victor and M. Villary, his former boss. Gisèle makes Mme Villary believe that her husband is having an affair with her and Mme Villary insists that her husband cut himself off from the theater at once. Unlike Victor, M. Villary is scrupulously honest, a quality not highly regarded in the world. When a man comes looking for a job at the theater, Victor treats him with extreme cordiality but does not give him work. M. Villary is quite gruff with him but gives him a job, and the man leaves complaining about M. Villary and praising Victor. Later, M. Villary loses all his money in an ill-advised investment in pharmaceuticals and becomes a bum. Victor runs across him and makes him his personal secretary, explaining to him that he must drop his glum and irascible manner and learn to smile all the time. M. Villary leaves behind his discourteous

Maurice Chevalier, in Maurice Tourneur's Avec le sourire, *flashes his famous smile, surrounded by the admiring women of the chorus line at the theater where he starts as doorman and soon becomes owner. Courtesy of Cinémathèque Française.*

ways, greets the world with a constant grin, and good fortune smiles on him once more.

Avec le sourire was one of a series of films Maurice Tourneur made in France during the 1930s, but as a director his reputation had been made long ago in America where, during the silent era, he was one of the pioneers. For a time head of the Eclair studios in New Jersey and Arizona, his early work was considered on a par with that of D. W. Griffith and Thomas Ince. Although his sound productions never equaled the sheer plastic beauty of his silent pictures, *Avec le sourire* has just enough satiric bite to make perfect use of Chevalier's malign good humor and to succeed where *L'Homme du jour* ultimately fails.

Abus de confiance

Abus de confiance presents a similarly cynical view of how to succeed in the calcified society of the 1930s. The heroine, Lydia, suffers a string of misfortunes at the beginning. He grandmother dies, leaving her alone in the world and bereft of all financial support. Paris is presented as an impersonal city full of men interested in taking advantage of her difficult situation. A well-dressed scion of the middle class sees her crying on a bench and tries to pick her up. She is refused service in her usual Latin Quarter restaurant because she has not paid her bill. The owner, who feels sorry for her, gives his waiter some money for her, but he keeps it. After the owner of her hotel tries to seduce her, she looks for work but the only person ready to hire her also wants to make love to her immediately, under a poster in his office that orders everyone to "consume." Another friend treats her to a meal, then tries to maneuver her right into a hotel room.

Having attempted to be honest, Lydia decides to play society's hypocritical game. Only after she passes herself off as the famous writer's illegitimate daughter are her material problems solved. By lying, she escapes from seedy hotels with threadbare furniture into a world of wealth and comfort. Her ruse works marvelously, bringing happiness to herself as well as the writer. Where integrity failed, she finds felicity through deceit.

The Role of Women

Both *Avec le sourire* and *Abus de confiance* give clear indication of the status of women in the society of the 1930s. Their position is basically subservient, vulnerable, and dependent on men. When Gisèle, taking a leaf from Victor's book, uses treacherous tactics to get rid of M. Villary and give her husband sole control of the theater, Victor is not pleased. He strongly disapproves of her employing his own base methods, which have the potential to make her self-sufficient. Early in her career, it is Victor/Chevalier who demonstrates to her the proper way to put over a song, although he is not a performer himself. Then, after making her a star, he insists that she retire from the stage and eventually she accedes to his wishes. Similarly in Pierre Caron's *Cinderella* (1937), a dancer who is the toast of Paris falls in love with an astronomer. Knowing he would strongly disapprove of her occupation, she keeps it a secret from him. He eventually finds out and demands that she choose between her career and him. After considerable hesitation, she opts for marriage. In *Abus de confiance,* Lydia at first finds herself reduced to such difficult straits that she is virtually at the mercy of the bevy of lechers ready to take advantage of her. She only escapes from their orbit by placing herself under the wing of another man, the eminent writer. For women, men represent at once the danger and the only salvation.

In *La Petite Lise,* Berthier's daughter is for many years, practically speaking, an orphan, and she turns to prostitution to support herself, replacing her real father with a sugar daddy. But even if she had found work, her salary would have been hardly enough to live on. Dressmakers and saleswomen were notoriously ill-paid. Demands for raises were often met with the suggestion that the workers moonlight in Lise's profession. For example, in May 1935 striking seamstresses demonstrating on the Champs-Elysées were told by the police, who brutally broke up the manifestation, to find lovers that would help make ends meet if their salaries were insufficient. A salesgirl, working in a department store in Montluçon and making only three hundred francs a month (about twenty dollars), complained to her boss that she could not live on her salary. His answer was "Look here, young lady, what do you do at night with your beauty?"[3] As far as the power structure was concerned, honest work did not necessarily spare a female employee from the need to double occasionally as a streetwalker. Dr. G. Paul-Boncour, a professor of criminology, found that "the percentage of prostitution caused by too low salaries and unemployment reached 40 percent of all prostitution in France."[4]

The idea of women as marketable commodities is made explicit in Pabst's *Le Drame de Shanghaï* and Pagnol's *Regain* ("Harvest") (1937). In the former film, the French reporter, Franchon, and his Chinese colleague have the following conversation, sitting at the bar of L'Olympique, watching the chorus girls perform: "Only today, it's these poor women who are in jail. But they can't escape." "Why?" "Because woman is a prisoner." The dancers are all Russian exiles who can find no other work and whose salary often supports their entire family. Nor does their job restrict itself to dancing. Any interested customer can get the telephone number of a performer who appeals to him from the club manager, Big Bill. When their act is over, Big Bill is waiting backstage to slap each one on the behind, and he becomes indignant when one protests, telling them they all danced like heavyweights (a term which applies better to him than to any of them). He adds, "And anyway, when you have thighs, you show them. You weren't hired for your talent." When he summarily fires the one dancer who refuses to put up with such insulting treatment any longer, another waif is waiting in the wings to take her job. There is more than a little irony in having a paunchy ex-convict, Big Bill, in charge of what is in reality a forced-labor situation, with a little sexual slavery mixed in.

Regain, based on a novel by Jean Giono, tells the story of the rebirth of a village, Aubignane, high in the Provence hills. Reduced to one last citizen, Panturle, it begins a new life when he finds a woman, Arsule, to share his austere existence there. Arsule, another piece of human jetsam who had been gang-raped by some woodcutters, had been in the company of a certain Urbain Gédémus (Fernandel), an itinerant sharpener of knives and tools, who had looked upon her much like a beast of burden. It was she who hauled his grinding wheel from town to town (he would only take over when they were close to villages, for appearances' sake). After she leaves him and becomes established in Aubignane, Urbain shows up one fine day to ask Panturle either for the return of Arsule or for compensation. When it becomes clear that he will not get her back, he puts the matter succinctly: "Since you want to keep the woman, give me a donkey." Although Panturle has enormous physical strength—he carried Arsule like a bride from the waterfall where they met to his village—he does not simply throw Gédémus out of his house. Instead, he reaches into the jar containing the money he and Arsule have so painfully acquired from a harvest of wheat that Panturle reaped by hand, opening long, gashlike blisters in his palms, and gives Gédémus enough money to purchase a donkey. Although Panturle and Arsule have developed a tender, loving, respectful relationship, he does not question Gédémus's premise that Arsule was his property, owned like the donkey he will buy. The equation of women and domestic animals could hardly be made more explicit.

La Maternité

One of the most extensive treatments of the disadvantageous position of women is found in Jean Choux's *La Maternité* (1934). In it, a young peasant, Marthe, has an illegitimate son which she gives up to the wealthy, childless couple for whom she works as a maid, so that the boy may enjoy the material and social advantages which she could never hope to give him.

At the beginning, Marthe, who is working at a mountain resort, gives in to the desire to take a nude swim in the cool waters of a lake. A wealthy young tourist happens by and seduces her. The entire sequence, which contains virtually no dialogue, gains much of its effect from Jacques Ibert's music, which unites the soft beauty of the countryside with the awakening of Marthe's emotions. It is seduction Victorian-style, resulting inexorably in pregnancy. She goes to tell the young man but cannot bring herself to interrupt the tennis game he is playing with well-to-do friends. She is subsequently fired because she is pregnant and is only restrained from hurling herself under an oncoming train by the cries of a child calling for its mother.

She goes to a different town, finds a room high up in a house, the position of which is established by a long, slow pan up the facade. Such garrets, providing the cheapest accommodations, were reserved for maids and other poor workers. Soon after, while doing laundry by hand on a *bateau-lavoir* on the river, she passes out and her son is born.

Subsequently, she goes to work for the Duchemins, a rich, insensitive couple who treat her like a subhuman. At first she is not even allowed to have her son living in their house with her. Later, when she obtains permission to do so, Choux juxtaposes shots of Marthe romping in her shabby bedroom with her little boy and of Mme Duchemin moping around her expensively appointed living room, sad because she has no child. Marthe and the boy have a close, loving relationship, the intensity of which is heightened by a striking, low angle shot in which she stands in a night dress holding him by candlelight, a genre scene worthy of Chardin. But although she almost runs away from the Duchemins to avoid giving up her son to them for adoption, a move they are pressing her to make, she finally disappears from his life until he reaches maturity.

He becomes an engineer and she comes across an article about him in the newspaper. Ironically, he looks exactly like his father (the two roles are played by the same actor, Henri Presles). She has had a bleak life in the meantime, filled with hard work and poor pay. Her son does not even know of her existence, having been too young at the time of his adoption to remember her. But she cannot resist the temptation to go and look at him from afar. Unfortunately, after she laboriously mounts a long, steep staircase, he accidentally runs her down. She is taken to the hospital where she dies happy, because he has come and kissed her, never realizing her true identity.

The sentimentality of the ending, which would certainly have delighted Diderot, only slightly softens what is otherwise an extremely cruel moral tale. A simple indiscretion is enough to bring down on Marthe the full wrath of an inflexible society's disapproval. Clearly, it does not pay to be poor. But even more distressing is the fact that her son does not really need her love at all. It is apparently far better for him to be raised by a selfish, superficial but affluent couple, bcause he reaches adulthood in splendid shape, emotionally, physically, and materially. In the end, Marthe is the victim of a rigorously paternalistic society, seduced by a debonair vacationer, then killed later, albeit accidentally, by his double. She is asked to sacrifice everything, getting only misery in return. That she can finally die happy is an eloquent indication of how oppressed she has been all of her life.

Marriage

In *Regain*, Pagnol shows how a relationship of love and respect can give people the strength to breathe new life into a village in the final stage of disintegration. The scene in which Panturle and Arsule are sowing together in the field expresses the theme in powerful terms. They walk toward each other, throwing wheat seeds on the ground, and as they pass in the middle, they exchange a look which communicates silently, against the background of Honegger's sweeping, lush, romantic music, their mutual understanding of the extraordinary bond that has developed between them.

In another film, *La Femme du boulanger* ("The Baker's Wife") (1938), Pagnol examines the opposite side of the coin, the difficulty in reconciling work and marriage. Two other important movies of the period explore similar terrain, Vigo's *L'Atalante* (1934) and Grémillon's *Remorques*, begun in 1939, interrupted by the outbreak of the war, and completed in 1941.

The plot of each picture is relatively simple. In *La Femme du boulanger*, the attractive young wife of a village baker, Aimable, runs off with a shepherd. Desolate, Aimable cannot bring himself to bake any more bread. In the true French manner, the villagers equate a total absence of bread with imminent starvation. Although they are usually feuding with each other, they forget their petty grievances in the face of such a crisis and band together to bring the errant wife back home, so that the furnace may be lit again.

In *L'Atalante*, a young village woman, Juliette, marries the captain of a river barge that plies France's inland waterways. But life aboard the boat proves boring and she slips off to spend a day in Paris, losing contact with the ship. After a harrowing separation, for both her and her husband, they are finally reunited.

Remorques tells of another captain, André Laurent, who commands a tugboat which rescues ships in distress at sea. In the course of saving a tanker during a storm, he meets a mysterious and fascinating woman with whom he falls deeply in love. He is unhappily married to a sick wife, whom he plans to leave for his new love. But before he can, his wife dies, and the object of his desire leaves, as abruptly as she appeared. He is left alone, except for his profession.

These three films are distinct in that they all accord a key narrative role to the trade of their central characters, a rarity in movies of the period. We have seen that in the boulevard comedies which comprise such a large portion of the 1930s films, work is rather a dirty word. The people in them are rich, but by some kind of divine right. Although passing reference may be made to the source of their affluence, a bank or a string of factories, they scrupulously refrain from the bad taste of working onscreen. Pagnol, Vigo, and Grémillon represent a diametrically opposite viewpoint. Their protagonists are average people who must depend on a job to earn a living. But their work does not simply provide a background for the plot; it is carefully integrated into the narrative structure so that it lies at the very heart of the marital problems the films explore.

In fact, in each film, it is through work that the third element of the triangle that threatens to break apart a fragile marriage is introduced. In *La Femme du boulanger*, the marquis introduces the theme of unmarried sex with the "nieces" who are permanent residents at his estate. The priest chides him for setting a bad example for the community but he maintains that sins requiring a substantial outlay of money cannot possibly tempt ordinary people. However, the actions of his shepherd, Dominique, to whom he assigns the task of picking up the bread for his household twice a week, do not bear him out. No sooner is Dominique in the bakery than he and the baker's wife, Aurélie, find themselves drawn together by a powerful physical attraction. Her husband, Aimable (Raimu), is so wrapped up in his trade that he notices nothing. He is an incredibly kind and generous, but asexual, person, with no inkling of unsatisfied longings stirring in his young wife's body. In bed, he is too busy calculating how much money he may make in his new shop to notice. He is even naive enough to think that the shepherd's serenade beneath their window is for him. When Aurélie steals off in the early hours of the morning, she leaves Aimable to sleep on while all his bread burns, for it is her task to wake him when it is time to remove the freshly baked loaves from the oven. Her departure comes as such a shock to Aimable that, while she is gone, he cannot bring himself to bake.

In *L'Atalante*, it is the peddler who serves as a disruptive force in the new but already tense marriage of Jean and Juliette. Juliette has, in an adventurous break with tradition, chosen to marry a man from outside the restrictive confines of her small Norman village. The very name of Jean's barge, *L'Atalante*, exudes mystery and excitement, and this is

Raimu, seated opposite Charpin, plays the drunk scene in Pagnol's La Femme du boulanger, *for which he improvised the running gag of the cigarette that never quite gets rolled or lit.*

what she seeks in her new life on board. Instead, she finds the ship's routine far more tedious than venturesome and, like Aurélie, she soon becomes bored with her marriage. Jean is usually busy running the boat, leaving Juliette to amuse herself most of the time. But, after she has washed Père Jules's mountain of dirty laundry, there is not all that much for her to do. Père Jules, with his cats and his bric-a-brac collected in the four corners of the world, is himself an exotic character who begins to capture Juliette's interest in a way that shows signs of becoming sexual. Jean, sensing this, orders her out of Père Jules's quarters in a fit of jealous pique and even breaks up some of the old man's souvenirs.

In the same way, he comes between Juliette and her desire for experience beyond the immediate scope of the barge. She is particularly anxious to become familiar with Paris, but Jean perceives this longing as a threat and arbitrarily turns off the Paris radio station she has been listening to with obvious fascination. Clearly Juliette expected *L'Atalante* to fill her life with a variety of exciting people and places; in her own small way, she is enchanted, like Marius, by what lies over the horizon. But the barge only touches port on the fringes of the cities, bleak, despondent, industrialized wastelands.

It is in just such a shabby backwater of Paris that the peddler suddenly appears. He is aggressive, fast-talking, full of tricks, interjecting some fun into her otherwise dull life. When Père Jules's drunkenness cheats her out of the trip into Paris she has been promised, Jean takes her to a local bistro as consolation. He disapproves of the peddler and is not pleased to find the man there, giving a brief performance as a one man band, walking on his hands, and hawking his wares. He sweeps Juliette away onto the dancefloor, while Jean sits glumly looking on. In his jealousy and authoritarianism, Jean has become increasingly rigid physically and his stiffness contrasts sharply with the peddler's extraordinary verbal and bodily flexibility. Juliette is quite taken with him, seeming to find in him the kind of dashing figure her husband no doubt used to cut before their marriage. Although Jean finally chases the peddler away from the barge and nothing develops between him and Juliette, he does appear to inspire her with some of his recklessness, giving her the courage to slip away on her own to Paris.

Although she finds the city dazzling at first, the move backfires when her purse is stolen and she is left destitute. When she fails to return on time, Jean, as if to teach her a lesson, casts *L'Atalante* off and heads for the next stop. But the separation proves as wrenching for him as for her. Like Aimable, without his wife he cannot work. He becomes distraught, neglects his job, does not shave, and drinks too much, to the point that he is almost fired. Meanwhile, the wife is forced to contend with depression conditions, scarce work, and long lines of the unemployed. Vigo intercuts shots of each of them tossing restlessly in separate beds to underscore their mutual loneliness. Finally, they are reunited through the good offices of Père Jules, who sees life aboard the barge deteriorating beyond repair.

In *Remorques* Captain André Laurent meets the mysteriously beautiful Catherine during a raging storm when he rescues her husband's boat. Catherine is everything that André's own wife, Yvonne, is not. Yvonne, played by Madeleine Renaud, is a homebody filled with anxiety when her husband goes forth into the teeth of storms to salvage sinking ships. As she tells the young bride of one of André's crewmen, whose wedding reception has just been interrupted by an S.O.S. "I'm alone . . . I'm sick . . . I'm afraid."[5] She clings desperately to her husband, sensing that he still seeks something she cannot give him. Catherine, in contrast, appears to fear nothing. Determined to leave her husband, she launches herself off from his ship in a dinghy into the full violence of the storm and is only saved by a miracle. Completely free and self-reliant, she asks nothing from André but a brief, intense affair. Beside her, Yvonne seems prosaic and predictable and André is ready to abandon his wife for his new love when Yvonne's weak heart gives out. Catherine, too, goes away, leaving him only his work, another storm, another rescue mission.

This narrative emphasis on the importance of work gives rise in each of the three films to a strong documentary element. *L'Atalante* contains a convincing portrayal of daily life aboard a river barge. *Remorques* depicts the way in which salvage crews operate, not only on deck in the fury of the storm, but in the engine room as well and, during a calmer period, in the galley, eating soup and round loaves of peasant bread. *La Femme du boulanger* not only takes us inside a bakery but also gives a portrait of a small Provençal village, its social hierarchy, and its petty disputes. Orson Welles admired the movie, and it is perhaps this aspect which appealed so strongly to him, since he was later to create a similar picture of a small Midwestern American town in *The Magnificent Ambersons*.

In each of the films, a close link is established between women and water. In *Remorques* Catherine is a creature of the sea. She likes storms, comes to André out of one, sweeping into his life like a swirling tide and departing just as abruptly. In one of the most striking sequences, she and André take a walk on a deserted beach, whose white sand has been bleached by salt and sun. Michèle Morgan, who plays Catherine, seems to possess a special kinship with the Breton seascape, with her pale skin, blond hair and Celtic ancestry. The starfish that she finds on the sand symbolizes her union with the sea in much the same way that Prévert, who wrote the dialogue, uses flowers as a symbol of Françoise in *Le Jour se lève* (1939). The starfish, which "They say allows lost sailors to get their bearings and find their way,"[6] will be the only tangible thing that remains to André of their love after Catherine is gone, when he will be most in need of a beacon to guide him.

The ocean, with its storms, boats, beaches, and fog, is the predominant image in *Remorques*, and in *L'Atalante* the rivers and canals, with their barges, wharves, locks, fog, their tree-lined banks, form an equally striking backdrop. Within this imagery, Juliette, who comes initially from land, becomes linked to water. During the separation, when *L'Atalante* comes into a seaport, Jean, beside himself, makes a desperate run to the edge of the ocean, as if he might find her there. She had once told him that if you look for the face of your beloved in water you will find her there. In another, lyrical sequence, he dives into the river and sees her underwater, looking blissfully happy in her wedding dress (in which, at the beginning, she appeared so apprehensive). She seems to have a special, almost parapsychological bond with the old seaman, Père Jules (who in fact consults a clairvoyante), which allows him to find her when she is staying alone at the Anchor Hotel, listening nostalgically to a sailor's song on a gramaphone. At the end, when the couple is reunited, the barge, seen from on high, sails off into the shining, shimmering waters of the river, the image of the perfect merging of their masculine and feminine natures.

In *La Femme du boulanger,* when Aurélie rides off with Dominique to quench her thirst for passion, it is to a place of water, the marshland, many of whose paths lie underwater, where it is dangerous to set foot without knowing the terrain, where the schoolteacher must carry the priest on his back to protect the cleric from the danger of drowning. In the film, however, water plays a secondary role to bread, another favorite symbol of Pagnol. Aurélie, like Arsule, her positive counterpart in *Regain*, is closely connected to this basic staple of nourishment, which remains intimately bound up with the cycles of nature. The first breaking of bread together is an important ceremony in the firm relationship developing between Arsule and Panturle, culminating in their first harvest and her pregnancy, and rejuvenating the dying village. When Aurélie comes home, Aimable shyly presents her with a loaf of bread shaped like a heart, which he says "just came out like that." Her presence, like Arsule's in Aubignane, will allow the village once again to resume its normal course.

The only French director of the decade who did not operate out of Paris, Pagnol took the profits from *Marius* and established his own studio, with a production, film processing, and distribution center in Marseilles. There he gathered around him a team of actors and technicians which made movies together like an extended family. Everyone worked together, ate together, and kept up a running discussion of the film in progress. Pagnol lived in the studio. The atmosphere was relaxed, free from the pressures of tight budgets. If a sequence came out badly, it was simply shot over again until it was good. For *Regain*, Pagnol reconstructed an entire village which had fallen into ruin. Honegger was present during the filming, often lending the crew a hand with its equipment, and composing the music with a firsthand idea of what each sequence required. Within this leisurely framework, *La Femme du boulanger* is unusual in that it was completed rapidly, in about three weeks, to fill an unexpected gap in the production schedule.

The circumstances under which Vigo and Grémillon worked were quite the opposite. *L'Atalante* was made on a minimal budget, which ran out with the scene in the railroad station still to be shot. Members of the Prévert brothers' leftist, avant-garde Groupe Octobre and other sympathetic friends donated their services as actors, so that the sequence could be made. Nounez, one of the co-producers, had delayed the start of filming until late fall, and the damp, frigid canals were too much for Vigo's health. He fell ill and, as he lay dying in the hospital, his film was butchered by the producers, who made cuts throughout and added a vacuous song which violated the film's intrinsic spirit. Understandably, it was a commercial failure. Vigo died on 5 October 1934; only many years later was his movie returned to a close approximation of the form he himself had envisaged for it.

Grémillon had arranged for the participation of the French navy to insure complete authenticity in the rescue scenes. Unfortunately, before a suitably violent storm struck the Brittany coast, World War II broke out, and Grémillon himself was mobilized. Actors and crew were scattered to the winds. Gabin, who played André with great authority, and Michèle Morgan both went to Hollywood, only resuming their European careers after the armistice. In order to finish the movie, Grémillon was obliged to resort to ship models and special effects, inevitably reducing the dramatic intensity of the salvage sequences.

Childhood

Zéro de conduite.   André Gide once remarked that children have been accorded a negligible role in the French novel. *Le Grand Meulnes* is an obvious exception and, in his presentation of *Zéro de conduite*, Vigo alludes to Alain-Fournier's masterpiece. Both the novel and the movie seek to recapture the fantasy world of children so often lost during the rite of passage into maturity. Both authors draw heavily on their childhood memories. Vigo wrote that "This film is so much my life as a kid that I'm anxious to move on to something else."[7]

Made under stringent budgetary restrictions which forced Vigo to cut the originally planned length in half, the film is set in a boys' boarding school and depicts the revolt of the students against the rigid discipline of the institution. It does not tell a story in the traditional sense, but presents instead a series of somewhat loosely related sketches of school life. As with *L'Atalante*, Vigo worked without benefit of an elaborate script, improvising scenes and dialogue as he went along, a technique which gives the film a narrative spontaneity that corresponds perfectly to the inner freedom of children which he sought to capture.

Vigo used professional actors for the school's staff, but for its students he selected boys who had never acted before, picking some from his neighborhood, following others he ran across in the street to sign them on, at the risk of being mistaken for a dirty young man. Before the camera, Vigo encouraged the boys to be as natural as possible, to simply play themselves, and he allowed them to improvise their own dialogue. Although handling the spirited, mischievous band of youngsters he collected put considerable strain on Vigo's fragile health, their collective performance gives the film a rare authenticity.

The son of a well-known anarchist, Almereyda, who died in prison under highly suspect circumstances, Vigo spent unhappy years as a boy at boarding schools in Millau and at Chartres similar to the one he portrays in the film. The four ringleaders of the revolt—Caussat, Bruel, Colin, and Tabard—are all modeled on school friends or on himself. The dormitory sleepwalker also comes directly from Vigo's personal experience, as do members of the school staff such as Huguet and Pète-Sec.

The children are full of a natural exuberance, whether they are blowing up balloons in imitation of women's breasts or pulling a fellow student off a toilet, pants down, into the school courtyard. Those who run the institution, with the exception of Huguet, exhibit uniformly repressive, hypocritical personalities stripped of any remnant of the passion for life so evident in their charges. The principal is a dwarf who rules the school with an iron hand but who is embarrassingly obsequious to the visiting prefect. His physical grotesqueness is matched by an ugliness of spirit, most apparent in the scene with Tabard when he explains, in a manic, incoherent way, his fears of homosexual interests in Tabard's older comrades. His assistant principal, Bec-de-Gaz, is equally unsavory, creeping silently, mysteriously, like a phantom, around the school, spying on the students, stealing candy from their desks, lurking about the latrines. Ironically, it is a faculty member, the slovenly, brutish chemistry teacher, who actually manifests an overt sexual preference for Tabard.

The mission of this repugnant crew is to stifle by the application of severe and arbitrary disciplinary measures, their students' inherent enthusiasm for life. Following Tabard's revolt against the school establishment, all the students' pent-up energy bursts forth in the dormitory.

The famous dormitory revolt scene in Vigo's Zéro de conduite.

The parade of the revolutionaries, shot in slow motion, expresses at once the boys' irrepressible spirit and their special world of fantasy. Suddenly braking the frenzied momentum of the pillow fight, Vigo captures a moment in which the boys' gestures abruptly become gentle. The air is filled with delicately falling feathers whose whiteness combines with that of the bedsheets and nightshirts to emphasize the essential purity of the young revolutionaries. The background music by Maurice Jaubert, a waltz, performed and recorded backward, then played back in its original order, heightens the strangely dreamlike quality of the scene.

Huguet is the link between the repugnant adult world and that of the children. He first appears in the railway car in which Caussat and Bruel return from vacation. He is hidden behind his overcoat and the boys choose to believe he is dead, an adjective that might aptly describe the emotional state of the school administrators. But he is only asleep, no doubt dreaming, as, with his distracted air, he almost always seems to be. This relationship in the compartment would seem to be the ideal one for Vigo, with adults and children occupied with their own business and neither infringing on the other's space. Unlike the other adults, much of the child lives on in Huguet, the amateurish imitator of Chaplin who stands on his hands when he is supposed to be supervising a study hall, and it is fitting that he later hails the students' disruption of the stilted

Alumni Day ceremony. As for the other adults, they are as bereft of life as the dummies in the stands at the *petite fête*.

It is possible to extend this devastating portrait of an inflexible, morally corrupt administrative hierarchy beyond the bounds of a small boarding school, to see in it an image of the whole of French society in the 1930s. This is exactly the correlation that the government made when it banned the commercial distribution of the film, which only gradually gained a loyal following through showings in cinema clubs. Society was not prepared to allow its mask to be torn away in public, especially by an anarchist's son advocating rebellion.

Poil de carotte. Duvivier's *Poil de carotte* (1932) portrays a family which also could be taken as a microcosm of a rigid, hypocritical society, a family so bereft of feeling that its youngest member is driven to attempted suicide. M. and Mme Lepic live together in mutual hatred. She has given her son, François, the insulting nickname of Poil de carotte (*poil* is the word for animal hair), because he is a redhead. She beats him and tries to stand between him and any pleasure, like going hunting with his father or dancing with the maid. At the same time, she lavishes affection on her spoiled, arrogant older son, who cares nothing for her and steals her money. M. Lepic is so alienated from the family that he seems to live off in his own world. At times he tries to show interest in his younger son, but the timing is usually bad and they fail to communicate. Nonetheless, the father is far from blameless. When he invites François to the celebration in honor of his election as mayor, he is too busy to spend any time with him there.

The film is set in the lush countryside surrounding Nevers, where the Lepics have a prosperous farm. The village is picturesque with its old fortress and could be paradise were it not for the boy's terrible family situation. His godfather, who tries to make up for the failings of François's parents, takes the boy on an idyllic outing one day, allowing him to fish, bath nude near a waterfall, and even take a sip of local firewater. Later François and a little friend, Mathilde, have a make-believe wedding and walk through a meadow with flowers in their hair, while the godfather plays an extraordinary instrument that resembles a viola, but makes music through a winding mechanism. But such magic times are all too rare, and the afternoon's freedom is brought to an abrupt end by a summons from his mother. On the way home in the wagon with the maid, the boy, frustrated by the sight of parents and children happily together in the fields and on the roads, drives the horse at breakneck speed, the trees racing by overhead.

Duvivier had already made a silent version of *Poil de carotte* in 1926, so that it is not surprising that the soundtrack plays an important part in the narrative. In the opening scene, M. Lepic comes downstairs into the living room, accompanied by a stream of hen-pecking from his wife, delivered voice-off. He pays no attention to it, never answers, simply shuffles off to go hunting. Only when he has left does the camera pan to reveal her standing in another area of the salon, clutching a prayer book. The yawning gap between them is abundantly clear again when the chiming of a clock interrupts the silence of a family meal. Later, when the boy leaves the celebration, says farewell to Mathilde, and goes home to hang himself in the barn, M. Lepic, alerted by the godfather, races desperately through the streets, followed by the sounds of the *fête*, of people singing, and bells ringing. When, unable to find François, he screams his son's name, the boy, the noose around his neck, covers his ears. But his father reaches him just in time. Afterward, they walk together in a field and truly communicate with each other for the first time. Duvivier intersperses their dialogue with shots of the tranquil, gentle countryside. As the father talks quietly to the boy, we see their reflections in the lake they pass near, a hay cart, hay fields, a close-up of wheat, then haystacks, until the camera finally returns to them again. Here, the voice-off technique is used, not to underline a separation, but, for the first time, a perfect harmony between people and their natural surroundings.

Harry Baur gives a strong performance as M. Lepic, but the most outstanding element of the film is Robert Lynan's portrayal of Poil de carotte, free of cuteness or annoying sentimentality. He acted in a number of other films before being captured by the Nazis, who shot him as a member of the resistance. Harry Baur died in a German concentration camp.

La Maternelle. *La Maternelle* (1933), by Marie Epstein and Jean Benoit-Lévy, takes us to an urban setting, to one of the poorest quarters of Paris. Benoit-Lévy felt strongly that the cinema had a responsibility to instruct as well as entertain, and it is not surprising that a number of his films are set in educational institutions. *La Maternelle* takes place in a kindergarten and revolves around the relationship between Rose, a well-educated young woman from an upper-class background who works as a maid at the school, and one of the students, Marie, whose mother, a prostitute, runs off with a wanted criminal. When Rose, who informally adopts the little girl, seems about to marry Dr. Libois, who oversees the kindergarten, Marie, believing that she is about to be abandoned again, tries to commit suicide, but, in the end, comes to accept the marriage. As in *Zéro de conduite* the children are presented without idealization, with a strong emphasis placed on their physical and emotional needs. They are shown sitting on toilets with Rose nearby to wipe their bottoms and button them up afterward. Mme Paulin, a maid with many years of service behind her, patiently picks lice from their hair. The conditions of their homelife seem uniformly appalling. One boy arrives at school with a black eye administered by his father. Another boy, Fondant, has never smiled until Rose coaxes a grin from him. Then one day, he does not appear; he has died. A father comes to the school drunk and blackmails a kiss from Rose in return for a promise not to beat his children when they get home, almost costing her her job. Marie's homelife is scarcely any better. Her father is not around and she lives in an apartment building where several whores openly ply their trade.

Marie shows the scars of this upbringing. Starved for affection, she purposely gets herself dirty so that Rose will help her clean up. When she is feeling shy, jealous, or upset, she stands with one shoulder hunched, and Rose must constantly remind her to hold herself straight. Like so many other central characters in films of the decade, she dreams of sailing off to another land and starting a new life. A local travel agency has a model of an ocean liner in its window which she loves to gaze at. It is after the doctor appears reflected in the window, in exactly the same way that her mother's lover had on the night her mother disappeared, that she goes to the river, spits on the image mirrored in the water of a couple embracing, and tries to drown herself. Only when she realizes that she will become part of the family is she reconciled to Rose's marriage.

Like Vigo, Epstein and Benoit-Lévy used only children without acting experience in the film. A large number were interviewed individually, to measure their "vivacity of spirit and degree of sensibility."[8] The selection of Paulette Elambert as Marie was inspired; her performance gives the film much of its impact. The movie was made in an actual kindergarten, in surroundings familiar to the children and in which they felt at ease. Their acting, like that of Vigo's older boys, is relaxed and natural. Marie Epstein was apparently extremely good at directing the children and inventing ways of bringing out the proper emotion in them, as when she threatened to break one of Paulette's dolls and was rewarded with a beautifully pained and fearful expression. The direction of Madeleine Renaud as Rose posed another problem. She was acting in a play by Alfred de Musset every night when the film was being made. A member of the Comédie Française, she brought before the camera a polished technique, yet what the directors hoped for from her was a performance as free from artifice as the children's. As she put it, "I understand. . . . You want me to forget my craft."[9] She successfully made the difficult transition each day from the sophisticated world of nineteenth-century comedy to the kindergarten.

Benoit-Lévy had his own small documentary film company and he approached the making of *La Maternelle* in the spirit of absolute authen-

In Marie Epstein and Jean Benoit-Lévy's La Maternelle, *Paulette Elambert pleads for the life of a rabbit at the working-class kindergarten in Montmartre. Courtesy of Cinémathèque Française.*

ticity. He and Marie Epstein lived for several months in kindergartens in the poor sections of the city, observing the children and familiarizing themselves with their attitudes. Many details, like the boy who never smiled, were drawn from real life. "We lived in these kindergartens which constitute a sort of paradise for children, an oasis of happiness for those among them, alas too numerous, who everywhere else know only misery and moral abandon."[10] Benoit-Lévy adds that he does not care to look for an excuse for the society which allows its children to grow up in such conditions of neglect. But the existence of their deplorable situation points vividly to a society far more interested in preserving the status quo than in coming to grips with its pressing problems, a society perhaps more fearful of change than of anything else, more intent on protecting privilege than of extending to all its members the opportunity to participate equally in the nation's wealth.

Benoit-Lévy had wanted to make *La Maternelle* for many years but had been turned down by scores of producers. When the completed film was first aired at a private showing the audience reaction was decidedly negative. Yet the public accepted it immediately, giving it an ovation at the première where, before the censor struck, it was to have shared billing with *Zéro de conduite*. Its great success both at home and abroad assured the directors a lavish budget for their next project, *Itto*. During World War II, Benoit-Lévy was forced to flee to America. The Germans destroyed all the prints of his films they could. He later became director of the film section at UNESCO, a fitting position for the man who considered the cinema to be as important an invention as printing.

Le Front populaire

Society's stubborn resistance to needed social change resulted in a political schism which polarized much of the country into right-wing and left-wing factions. On the right, a number of reactionary organizations were active, the most archaic of which was the Action française, from which even the Catholic church had withdrawn support. The Croix de feu, a group of ex-servicemen headed by Colonel de la Rocque, saw its membership grow prodigiously during the decade. Other, smaller units like the Jeunesses patriotes and the Solidarité française, the latter founded and funded by the perfume millionaire Coty, also worked to stir up conservative sentiment, much of which was nationalistic and anti-Semitic. The violence of the fascist thugs who disrupted the showing of *L'Âge d'or*, screaming "Death to the Jews!" was widespread in the streets. Vendors and distributors of *L'Humanité*, the communist party newspaper, and of leftist leaflets were routinely set upon by gangs of right-wing hoodlums armed with canes used as clubs, who were, if caught, treated lightly by the courts. On 3 February 1936, Léon Blum himself had the misfortune to be driving by a funeral procession for Action française historian Jacques Bainville. Catching sight of the Jewish socialist, the grief-stricken mourners dragged him from the vehicle, slugged and stomped him, while a woman in a fur coat screamed, "Kill him!"[11] There is reason to believe they would have, had some workers from a nearby construction site not intervened. That a member of the Chamber of Deputies could be assaulted at noontime on the Boulevard Saint-Germain is a clear indication of how dangerously explosive the political situation had become.

During this period of political, economic, and social unrest, governments fell with alarming regularity. The Stavisky affair in 1933 brought down the Chautemps cabinet. Stavisky, a con-man with influential friends both within the police and the government, floated millions of francs worth of valueless bonds backed only by the modest municipal pawnshop of Bayonne. The scandal, when it broke, not only touched off a round of ministerial resignations but indirectly inspired the failed right-wing coup d'état of 6 February 1934, which in turn toppled the Daladier government.

It was against this background of political instability and violence on the right, that the various factions of the French left joined together to forge the loose coalition of radicals, socialists, and communists known as the Front populaire, which came to power in the general elections of 1936.

Renoir's *La Vie est à nous*, made as a propaganda piece to rally electoral support for the Front populaire, intentionally underscores the widening rent in the French social fabric. Produced by the Communist party, the film combines contemporary documentary footage with fictional episodes, blending actual speeches by communist dignitaries like Maurice Thorez with invented anecdotes like the story of René, the unemployed engineer. Its aim is to express convincingly and persuasively the leftist point of view, and for this reason it does not have, nor need, a plot in the traditional sense.

In addition to scenes of daily life such as a group of right-wing heavies leaning on a seller of *L'Humanité* and lines of people out of work waiting to be fed at free soup kitchens, it depicts clearly the hostile gulf between the upper and lower classes. There is a sequence of pages from an album containing pictures of members of the two hundred families reputed to control the finances of France, some with familiar names like Renault, later to be stripped of its auto company in 1945 for having collaborated with the Nazis. In the words of the film's chorus, "France does not belong to the French / Because it belongs to the 200 families."[12] Resentment against them ran so high that, while the Front populaire was in power, the names of the 200 families were routinely read out at the entrance to metro stations.

In another section set on the grounds of a chateau, the enmity between classes is illustrated in more graphic terms. Near a lake with
swans and peacocks, a locale that calls to mind Archibald's estate in *Ma
cousine de Varsovie,* a group of rich young men take target practice at a
line of human dummies. A young woman appears with a cap to be placed
on the head of one of the targets. Since the cap was the symbol in the
1930s of the working class, some of whose unemployed members are
calling out for work and bread from outside the chateau's iron fence, the
shooters are delighted. "Oh! marvelous. A real *salopard's* cap!"[13] Workers, too, are *salopards,* the kind of throwaway human trash routinely
eradicated in colonialist films for the national good. After the addition of
the cap, the marksmanship becomes inspired. The group at the chateau
is linked together in a montage to another band of fascists dressed in the
blue shirts and berets of Marcel Buccard's Francistes, an organization
which was later to collaborate with the Germans during the occupation.
The beret, sported by Pierre Tattinger of the champagne family when he
founded the Jeunesses patriotes, had become the symbol of the militant
right, and the subject of a running joke in the Prévert brothers' *L'Affaire
est dans le sac* (1932). The montage of fascists is completed by a parade of
the Croix de feu, with the Colonel de la Rocque in the lead, his
movements altered so that he seems to be doing an absurd dance. His
image is quickly replaced by Hitler's and then Mussolini's, two leaders
whose rise to absolute power many felt de la Rocque sought to emulate.
Later, when René, the down-and-out engineer, finally finds a job wash-
ing cars, he is sacked the same day because of the complaint of a
well-heeled young member of the Croix de feu whose car is not quite
ready when he comes to pick it up. And when René faints from hunger in
the street, a bourgeois lady immediately assumes that he is just another
working-class drunk.

The making of *La Vie est à nous* was carried out in a cooperative spirit.
Although Renoir oversaw the project, other directors actually were in
charge of filming certain sections. Jacques Becker shot the farm auction
scenes, Jean-Paul Le Chanois the transition sequences, and Jacques-
Bernard Brunius handled the documentary footage. The three also act in
the film. Actors, directors, and technicians donated their services, so
the movie cost about one tenth of the average budget for a feature film at
the time, and it was financed by contributions from members of Ciné
Liberté, an organization created to fund the project. This same attitude
of joining forces for the common good forms the essence of another
Renoir film, *Le Crime de Monsieur Lange* (1935).

Le Crime de Monsieur Lange relates how the workers in a publishing
house take over the running of the business on a cooperative basis when
the owner, M. Batala, a kind of small-time Stavisky, gets way in over his
head with creditors and is obliged to disappear for a while. The workers
turn the nearly bankrupt operation into a prosperous enterprise, thanks

to the literary talents of one of them, Amedée Lange, who writes best-selling Westerns. When Batala returns and wants to take over again, Lange, taking a page from the book of his hero, Arizona Jim, guns down his former boss and escapes across the Belgian border with Valentine, the woman he loves.

The communal spirit in both films infuses them with a vibrant feeling of optimism that ordinary people working together can take charge of their own lives and bring about effective change, even in the face of the most difficult circumstances. The way in which the workers salvage the publishing house finds its parallel in the farm auction scene in *La Vie est à nous*. Creditors have foreclosed on a farmer, forcing the sale of his furniture and equipment. But a communist nephew and his friends make sure nobody else bids on any of the goods, which they are then able to buy for a pittance and return to the uncle.

In both films the cooperative energy embraces both men and women. In *La Vie est à nous*, both sexes join in the final apotheosis, chanting the refrain "Life belongs to us." The action of *Le Crime de Monsieur Lange* centers around the courtyard that houses not only the publishing company but also a laundry, run by Valentine, and staffed by women. Throughout the movie there is a constant interplay and feeling of unity between the two businesses which parallels the love between Lange and Valentine.

Batala, stunningly portrayed by Jules Berry, is a monster of deception and exploitation who makes a whore out of a woman who loves him, then abandons her to her new profession and who automatically smooth-talks the naive Lange out of the rights to his novel. He is like the rich industrialist in *La Vie est à nous*, played by Brunius, who insists at a board meeting that workers must be made to sacrifice, then later loses a million francs at a casino without a second thought. The message of *Le Crime de Monsieur Lange* is that such economic parasites deserve to be shot, for, although it is Lange who pulls the trigger, his killing is very much a communal meting out of justice. Unlike Legrand, his dreamy, artistic counterpart in *La Chienne*, Lange does not kill for personal reasons but to save the cooperative. He shoots Batala, who is still impersonating a priest, in the courtyard, and the 360 degree pan which precedes his act has the effect of drawing all those who live and work there into the murder. In this respect, it is significant that early titles considered for the film were "Sur la cour" and "Dans la cour."

Like René in *La Vie est à nous*, Lange represents a welding together of the intellectual and the working classes of the kind represented by the Groupe Octobre, whose members participated actively in the making of both movies. René is an engineer, Lange a writer; René throws his lot in with the Communist party, Lange with the cooperative. His very name, a play on the French word for angel (*l'ange*) and laundry (*linge*), symbolically links him and his destiny to Valentine's establishment, the only other business in the courtyard. When he decides to escape, both leave their respective enterprises and head for the Belgian border, where an ad hoc court of customs officials and border guards, an ordinary jury of Lange's peers, decide to let him pass unhindered to freedom, a decision which places them in solidarity with the workers in the courtyard.

Another film which gives eloquent expression to the optimistic *élan* of the early days of the Popular Front alliance is Duvivier's *La Belle équippe* (1936). It follows the fortunes of five unemployed workers who together buy a lottery ticket and win 100,000 francs. They decide to use their winnings to start a restaurant on the banks of the Marne. They buy a big old house which has fallen into disrepair, but, as they fix it up, their association, initially so firm, gradually falls apart. By the time the inn is ready to open, the group has been reduced from five to two members, both of whom are attached to the same woman.

Especially at the beginning, the film is imbued with the spirit of workers banding together in an attempt to better their lot. Duvivier first portrays the plight of the unemployed men who, flat broke, can only gaze longingly at a poster extolling the fun to be had in Gay Parée but who must play cards by candlelight when their electricity is cut off. Then, when the news of their good luck breaks, their seedy hotel suddenly comes alive with excitement as they buy drinks for the other guests, delighted at their sudden prosperity. As a sign of their new status, the proprietor brings them clean sheets, a luxury reserved for the rich at a time when two thirds of the dwelling places in France had neither running water nor sanitary installations.

The spot they pick for their restaurant is an idyllically pastoral setting, and Duvivier includes some striking footage of the sun glistening on the water and through the leaves of the trees and of boaters on the Marne very reminiscent of impressionist canvasses. After the grimy streets of Paris it seems like an earthly paradise and, in fact, one of the five suggests calling their inn "Le Paradis." Another wants to name it "Chez Nous," as a sign of the cooperative nature of the enterprise. A third jokingly proposes "La République," where everyone is president, accenting the populist tone of the undertaking. The rustic locale parallels a fresh interest in the outdoors and in healthy recreation generated by the Popular Front government and the labor reforms ratified in the Matignon Accords of 7 June 1936. Léo Lagrange, head of the newly created Office of Sports and Leisure, actively encouraged physical fitness, hiking, and skiing. The widespread strikes that greeted the coming to power of the *Front populaire* resulted in important improvements in working conditions, notably a forty-hour work week and two weeks of

The grand opening of the dance hall in Julien Duvivier's La
Belle équipe, *an ordinary people's* fête champêtre, *evoking the
spirit and atmosphere of the Popular Front. Courtesy of
Cinémathèque Française.*

paid vacation, which gave the industrial laborers the time and money to
explore, for the first time, the French countryside. "Thanks to the
forty-hour week, couples on tandem bicycles could now be seen pedal-
ing out of Paris every Saturday morning; they came back on Sunday
evening with bunches of flowers and foliage tied to their handlebars."[14]

The unity and determination of the group reaches its zenith during a
sudden night storm in which the new tiles on the roof they have been
rebuilding begin to blow away. The five climb up onto it in a fierce wind
and torrential rain and, stretched out, lying flat, their hands clasped,
singing to keep up their courage, they manage to keep most of the roof
intact.

Within this Popular Front atmosphere the film combines certain
dominant themes of the decade, in particular those of urge to travel and
of male companionship. One of the five, Jacques, dreams of sailing off to
Canada to start a new life in a new land. He is the first to break the bond
of the unit, partly because he gives in to Marius's old desire, but even
more so because he is hopelessly in love with the wife of Mario, another
of the partners. Mario's wedding early in the film had been a joint
celebration for the group, coinciding with the winning of the lottery.

While several members filched token presents for the couple from a machine while the proprietor was not looking, another brought Mario's fiancée to him through the streets of Paris on a bicycle. Since Mario is Portuguese, a political exile from the Salazar regime who has already been hounded out of several other countries and whose days in France seem numbered, their marriage represents an unusually strong commitment and they are very much in love. Rather than violate this union, Jacques quietly slips away. Later Mario is indeed obliged to leave France.

Later, Charles' wife, Gina, who had left him when he was broke, reappears. Having little love for her husband but considerable interest in his money, she quickly sees that the firm friendship of the men represents an obstacle and sows dissension among them by seducing Jean (Jean Gabin). By the time the problem comes to a head, of the original five only Jean and Charles remain, although Jacques has kept in touch with nostalgic letters that help bolster the resolve of those he left behind. The third to go, Raymond, dies in a fall when the remodeling is finished and during the celebration he tipsily places "the flag of the workers" on the roof.

The film had two different endings. In one, preferred by Duvivier, comradeship turns to hatred, and Jean kills Charles on the day the restaurant opens. As in *Légions d'honneur*, in which Charles Vanel again plays a husband who loses the affections of his wife to his best friend, a woman comes between two close friends. The producer did not like this grim denouement and insisted that Duvivier film a happy one in which Jean breaks with Gina, telling his friend, "There are things between us which are worth more than a woman." Male friendship and the enterprise triumph.

Despite capturing the atmosphere of the times with unusual accuracy, and the tacking on of a saccharine ending, the movie was not a great success commercially. It did, however, give Viviane Romance her first major role, launching her sometimes stormy career during which she was extremely popular with moviegoers and ignored by the critics. Since the film was a logical sequel to *Le Crime de Monsieur Lange*, Renoir was extremely anxious to make it, but Duvivier was unwilling to relinquish his option. Instead, Charles Spaak, the scriptwriter for *La Belle équipe*, collaborated on the screenplay for *La Grande illusion* with Renoir, which became the most popular work in the director's long career.

In Duvivier's first ending, after shooting Charles, Jean repeats, "It was a beautiful idea. A beautiful idea that we had. . . . Too beautiful, certainly, to succeed."[15] His words could also serve as an epitaph for that equally fragile alliance, the Front populaire. As soon as the Blum government assumed office, it was beset by grave problems. In June

1936 over 12,000 strikes swept across the country, with workers occupying many factories, including the film studios at Billancourt and Joinville, and those of Pathé. In July, the Spanish Civil War broke out and Blum's policy of nonintervention did much to dissipate the momentum of the movement. Numerous right-wing journals kept up a constant stream of polemic against government policies, criticizing especially the Exposition of 1937 which was to be the showpiece of the coalition. Utterly slanderous and vituperative attacks on the character of Roger Salengro, the minister of the interior, in the rightist newspaper *Gringoire* drove him to commit suicide. Then, a Popular Front counter-demonstration to one held by members of the Croix de feu in the working class suburb of Clichy was broken up by the forces of law and order who fired on the crowd, killing 5 and wounding 200, including André Blumel, Blum's *directeur du cabinet*, who was attempting to restore order, and this, too, seemed to snap something in the movement's spirit. French cardinals joined together in a pastoral letter to denounce the Popular Front. Financial problems largely inherited by Blum became so acute that even a devaluation of the franc had little impact on them. And in June 1937, "For all its excessive prudence, Blum's cabinet fell, brought down by the banks, railway companies and big insurance groups."[16]

Moving Toward War

If French society of the 1930s was one of masks, it is not surprising that the facade plays a prominent part in the decor of its films. In *Abus de confiance*, for example, when the heroine, Lydia, runs out of the courthouse in distress, she is greeted by a montage of impersonal, empty-looking building fronts. *Derrière la façade* (1939) offers to take us behind one of these faceless exteriors and give us a glimpse of the people who live there, a kind of microcosm of a society in a state of advanced decomposition.

The film, by Yves Mirande and Georges Lacombe, follows the police inquiry into a murder committed in a Parisian apartment house, in the course of which we come to know all the inhabitants. They present a bizarre mix, including a drunken knife thrower with an understandably nervous wife-assistant; a kleptomaniac who steals one of his performance weapons; a bed-ridden old man whose daughter has sold off his painting collection to pay the household bills without her father knowing, while her boy friend lifts money from his employer's till to help her pay the rent; an elegant idler (Jules Berry) who, on being led into an area he never needs to visit, remarks with lofty indignation, "What's this?? A kitchen??!! I abhor kitchens!"; an important political figure who is having a clandestine affair with a singer whom his son tries to buy off; the murder victim, a rapacious old lady who owns the building and who was not above a little high-class pimping; and the killer, her equally old, ill-paid, and ill-treated concierge.

Perhaps the most interesting tenant is a shady German (Eric von Stroheim), who has just been naturalized a French citizen on the morning of the murder. He has nothing but arrogant scorn for a French business associate from whom he has just won a great deal of money at cards. He refuses to cut the Frenchman in on the profits of a questionable deal which the latter helped set up and cavalierly gives a large chunk of his gambling proceeds to his opponent's mistress. When the two quarrel, the German easily overpowers his erstwhile partner, further humiliating him in front of his lady friend. The police arrive during the scuffle and the German immediately complains that they are handling him disrespectfully, archly informing them that he has friends in high places. The inspectors are unimpressed, even downright hostile: "If you don't like the way you're being treated, all you have to do is get yourself renaturalized in your own country." The scene underscores a current of xenophobia running throughout the decade, directed most often at Jews or Germans, foreigners frequently perceived as appropriating money and jobs which otherwise would go to the French.

This strain of sentiment appears also in Renoir's *La Règle du jeu* (1939), in which Robert de la Chesnaye, the marquis who owns the chateau where most of the action takes place and has a Jewish maternal grandfather, is characterized by his chauffeur as a *métèque*, a pejorative term for undesirable aliens. In the film, La Chesnaye invites a group of upper class friends to his estate for a hunting party. During an evening *fête* the amorous escapades of his guests and those of his servants break out into violence, culminating in the death of André Jurieu, an aviator and national hero.

Renoir set out to paint "an exact description of the bourgeoisie of our time."[17] He began work in the shadow of the Munich agreement, intending to portray a society that was, as he put it, gnawed by a malady and "dancing on a volcano."[18] For inspiration, he reached back to the eighteenth century, to Beaumarchais and Marivaux (his first working title for the movie was "Les Caprices de Marianne") and also to the romantic playwright Alfred de Musset.

The setting he chose, very much in the spirit of those mentors, is a familiar one; we have seen it already in *Ma cousine de Varsovie*. Many of the characters, too, are, in a sense, old friends: the wealthy industrialist whom we never see at work, and other rich denizens of the upper reaches of society whose lives consist purely of leisure time spent gossiping, playing cards, and pursuing other peoples' spouses. In fact, it is against the backdrop of the *cinéma de boulevard* which so dominated the output of the decade that Renoir's originality may best be appreciated, for he takes all the ingredients of a genre intended to provide light, comfortable, reassuring, escapist entertainment and turns them into a scathing portrait of a sick society. Renoir does not present the rich as admirable, nor does he consider their vacuousness exemplified by Mme La Bruyere's belief that pre-Columbian art consists of "des histoires de nègres," simply a pretext for innocent, indulgent humor.[19] And their amorous dalliance, no longer idle diversion which resolves itself cleanly at the end, is a source of unpleasant tension which the death of Jurieu augments rather than dissipates.

According to Renoir, the basis on which society rests is one of deception: "Listen Christine, that too, it's a thing of our epoch! We're in an epoch where everyone lies: pharmaceutical prospectuses, governments, radio, movies, newspapers. . . ."[20] The biggest lie is, of course, La Chesnaye's explanation of Jurieu's killing, which he passes off as an accident, in a way that confirms the general's oft-repeated assessment that his host is one of those rare people that still has class. But the compliment, sincerely meant, is a hollow one. La Chesnaye is a hopelessly frivolous type whose greatest passion is for elaborate mechanical musicmakers like the organ he so proudly unveils at the *fête*. He cuts a rather ridiculous figure when, in an attempt to hang onto his wife, he fights Jurieu, while one of his servants runs amok. He arranges a hunt in which he and his sophisticated guests, with almost inhuman calm and propriety, slaughter a sickening number of rabbits and pheasants. And, although he supposedly finds it impossible to lie, he does an excellent job of it in a very delicate situation, justifying the general's high esteem.

Unlike the servants of Beaumarchais, those of Renoir are a source of neither wisdom nor strength. They are, in the end, no better than their masters, whom they admire and mimic. Lisette's only real attachment is to her mistress, Christine; her husband, Schumacher, is a jealous, dangerous blockhead with fascist overtones, and Marceau's greatest wish is to give up his poacher's freedom and become a servant. Thus the social illness has spread like a cancer from top to bottom, making the dance of death performed at the *fête* a fitting image for the whole of French society on the eve of war.

At its premiere, the film was greeted by a violent audience reaction which ran from boos and hisses to the destruction of the theater seats. The spectators recognized all too clearly their own reflection on the screen and were in no mood to tolerate being unmasked at a time when their whole world seemed on the verge of collapse. France was now encircled by fascist dictatorships in Germany, Italy, Spain, and Portugal. Its position in Europe was perilously weak: "And so the real news emerges—that France's finances are in a terrible way, and that Paris, once the leader of Europe, dare not risk even verbally offending neighbors whom she formerly deigned to insult by battle."[21] The nation's last hope lay in its alliance with England, the strategic importance of which was emphasized in L'Herbier's *L'Entente cordiale* (1939), a tedious but highly appreciated evocation of the Fashoda Affair and the subsequent Franco-British rapprochement. The visit of King George VI and Elizabeth of England to Paris in 1938 inspired an outpouring of public enthusiasm greater than that of their coronation in London. Another event, the execution of Weidmann, a German murderer, produced such a festive atmosphere at Versailles, where the cafés stayed open all the night before with jazz blaring forth on the radios, that the minister of justice passed a decree banning public executions in the future. At the Théâtre-Français, a revivial of *Cyrano de Bergerac*, with Rostand's witty, invincible national hero, was a smash hit. In this tense, anxious atmosphere, *La Règle du jeu*, which had been roundly panned in *Gringoire*, was declared demoralizing by the military censor withdrawn from circulation. At a time when "The part played by the journalists of the right, many of whom ended as collaborators of the Nazis in the Second World War, in sapping the moral fibre and powers of resistance of the Third Republic can hardly be exaggerated," a steady stream of leftist films fell under the axe of the censor, among them *Pépé le Moko*, *Quai des brumes*, *Le Jour se lève*, and *Le Crime de Monsieur Lange*.[22] *Quai des brumes*, with its deserter hero, was even declared by various spokesmen of the Vichy government to have singlehandedly brought about the defeat of France. It was the Germans, however, who finally reduced the art of censorship to absurdity by banning Christian-Jaque's *Rigolboche* (1936). They prohibited this innocuous musical comedy, starring an amazingly well-preserved Mistinguett who in earlier times had performed at the original Moulin Rouge, because they assumed from the title that it was a film making fun of Germans. *La Vie est à nous* was never even submitted to the board of censors in the 1930s, since it was believed to have no chance of passing. Its commercial career began in 1968, in the Studio Gît-le-Coeur, following another moment of populist solidarity, the student uprisings of May. It was also in the 1960s that *La Règle du jeu* was finally reissued in a form close to Renoir's original conception and slowly began to find the devoted audience it merited.

5

Saturday Night at the Movies

Un Carnet de bal

WHILE FILMS that too closely reflected the decaying society of the time faced banning by censors, charming, nonpolitical vehicles for popular performers flourished. Early in the 1930s in France, a vast number of people, many of whom worked on Saturday and did not have much money to spend on entertainment, got into the habit of going to the movies on Saturday night for recreation, a custom which grew into a social ritual: "The Saturday night movie was an outing for the gang, an outing for couples, an outing for the family, rarely, almost never, the solitary disarray of the spectator without friends, without love, or without hope: you would always meet or run into someone. . . ."[1]

It was a decade during which the actor was king. Often the signing of a star was sufficient to obtain financing for a project—Gabin for *Quai des brumes*, for example—whose details were still extremely vague. Marc Allégret had a knack for sensing tremendous potential in little-known players and for giving them the roles which established them as *vedettes*. Simone Simon in *Lac aux dames* (1934) and Michèle Morgan in *Gribouille* (1937) were two such discoveries. So magnetic a drawing force were actors that a number of films, like *Derrière la façade*, were built around an all-star cast. One of the most memorable of these productions was Duvivier's *Un Carnet de bal* (1937).

The film, whose formidable cast includes Harry Baur, Louis Jouvet, Fernandel, Raimu, Pierre Blanchar, Françoise Rosay, and Marie Bell, has a narrative construction novel for the time, a series of related sketches rather than a continuously developed plot. In it, a young widow, Christine, comes across the dance card of her first ball when she was sixteen and decides to look up her old partners and see what has become of them. The settings of the individual segments present a series

Marie Bell clutches the dance card of her first ball, as romanticized dancers, silhouetted against the background, rise up from her memory in Julien Duvivier's Un Carnet de bal. *Courtesy of Cinémathèque Française.*

of sharp contrasts, moving from a grieving mother's solitary apartment to a nightclub, to a monastery, to the Alps, to a sunny southern village, to the grimy port of Marseilles, and finally to the town where the ball originally took place.

Although the episodes are uneven in quality, the film is both visually and aurally interesting throughout. At the outset, Duvivier establishes a tone of mystery, an almost fairy-tale atmosphere. The opening shot is a pan of a still lake with mountains in the background. Then, from a distance, through the arch of a small bridge, we see a boat approach, which the camera picks up and follows. In it are two dark figures, one of whom is clothed in a hooded cape. We do not know who they are, nor can we even be sure of their sex. As their boat docks and they climb the steps to a chateau, there is no dialogue to distract from the spectacular beauty of the surroundings or to dispel the enigma of their identities, only the crunch of their footfalls on the gravel. Not until they are within the castle do we learn that it is Christine and a friend returning from her husband's funeral. The sequence establishes an ambiance of fantasy which prepares us psychologically for Christine's fanciful remembrances of things past.

The discussion between Christine and her friend of her future options moves from the window at which they are standing, to the dinner table and then, when the meal is finished, to the piano. It is a relatively brief dialogue which extends over a period of hours, a dislocation in time which further sets the stage for her dreamlike foray into the past.

Her memories of her first ball, triggered by the dance card, begin with the notes of a waltz which starts up delicately. The camera draws back from her and, as the music grows more sonorous, the scene of the *bal* gradually begins to superimpose itself over the salon in the chateau, until it takes over the screen completely. In her recollection, the evening appears full of excitement and elegance. The waltz is refined, graceful, and romantic, the ballroom tastefully opulent. The young women are clad in gowns of white, their male counterparts in formal attire. The sequence is filmed in slow-motion: the girls bow, the young men run across the floor to their partners, and the couples waltz in a circle. As in the dormitory revolt in *Zéro de conduite,* the device gives an air of reverie to the action. This feeling is reenforced later in her bedroom when the memories come flooding back and the dancers are silhouetted against the gauzelike window curtains, the waltz music again in the background. As in *Zéro de conduite,* Jaubert recorded the waltz, rerecorded it backward, then played it back in its original order of notes, a technique which further infuses the scene with an atmosphere of unreality. Later, at the end, when she returns to the actual location of the dance, Christine is amazed to find, instead of the ballroom she remembered as so splendid, a drab and seedy place, badly decorated, in which the couples seem shabbily provincial. Just as the room loses its charm, so does the waltz become graceless and vulgar, underscoring the disillusioning gap between memory and reality.

A far grimmer brand of realism prevails in what is perhaps the most striking sketch, in which she visits the dancing partner (Pierre Blanchar) who has become an illegal abortionist. He plies his trade in a low-rent apartment near the Marseilles docks where no music is heard, only the ear-splitting din of a loading crane. A doctor who has sunk to the lowest depths of his profession, he has lost the sight of one eye thanks to a virulent drop of pus and has brought a case of epilepsy with him back from the tropics. When Christine enters, oblivious to what she is saying, he mistakes her for a client and mechanically begins to take out and disinfect the instruments of his calling. To convey the hellishness of his existence in the sordid flat, Duvivier makes effective use of oblique camera angles, catching within the tilted frames snatches of a world gone awry. Contact with Christine makes him dream briefly of starting anew, but his vitriolic wife quickly dashes these fragile hopes, driving him to murder her. Her cries for help and the revolver shot are drowned out by the infernal clatter of the crane.

Pierre Blanchar's piercing eyes, his haunted look, his intense, smoldering style of acting meshes perfectly with the nightmarish atmosphere of the episode. Yet surprisingly, considering the impressive cast, the other performances are by no means uniformly distinguished. Harry Baur, who had given such a rousing, thoroughly convincing performance in the title role of Alexis Granowsky's *Tarass Boulba* (1936), is too low-key, too tranquil as the monk who has renounced the world and its ambitions. Fernandel, also, is mediocre. As the Alpine rescue specialist, Pierre-Richard Willm is extremely weak. The segment's interest is strictly visual: stunning footage of an avalanche and of the soaring, white mountains. In one particularly effective sequence two skiers (Christine and the Alpinist) appear first as two small figures in the lower right corner of the frame, dwarfed by the imposing, alabaster slope they are descending, then swoop down to fill the screen.

Françoise Rosay, who got her first break as a film actress in Hollywood when she was there with her husband, Jacques Feyder, in the late 1920s, gave one of the finest performances by an actress in the 1930s as Louise Noblet in Feyder's *Pension Mimosas*. Feyder has recorded how attentive she was to her craft, how she would carry on a minute documentation on each role, choosing all the details of her costumes and accessories, how she would arrive at the studio on the first day with her lines memorized and mastered. Yet here, unfortunately, none of this pays off. As the bereaved and mentally unbalanced mother, she overacts, making her work come across as artificial and stilted.

Far and away the most powerful performance is given by Louis Jouvet in a role which bears resemblance to his later characterization of Ivan in *Le Drame de Shanghaï*. Here he plays a disbarred lawyer who manages a night club and runs a band of thieves on the side, using his legal expertise to evade the law. This formerly timid suitor of Christine, who used to cite Verlaine to her on the shore of a lake, has become a study in dissipation. A student of the penal code who keeps nude photographs in his desk, he is intent upon robbing a blind baron with a prurient interest in one of the young girls in the club. Like his medical counterpart, he does not at first recognize Christine and can only imagine two possible reasons for her arrival at his *boîte:* either she has come to sleep with him or to borrow money—perhaps both. His speech is laced with *argot* and he walks slowly, as if drugged by licentiousness and decay. Yet he still exhibits great strength and power of command over the three hoodlums who follow his orders. Not quite well enough, unfortunately, for all four are apprehended at the end. The police arrest Jouvet at the bar where, once again, he is reciting Verlaine to Christine. He is led away across the club floor, his gait that of a somnabulist, anaesthetized by degradation.

Un Carnet de bal, which won the prize as the best foreign film at the Venice film festival of 1937, was an immense success. Janet Flanner called it "one of the major films the French have ever made" and Duvivier "the number-one French studio chief today."[2] Jaubert's *valse grise* also became an instant hit, passing directly into the popular song repertory, like the lively waltz he had composed for Clair's *Le Quatorze juillet* (1932). With *Un Carnet de bal* Duvivier set the standards for films made up of sketches, a form to which he returned in Hollywood during the war with *Lydia* (1941), *Tales of Manhattan,* and *Flesh and Fantasy* (1943), working with a galaxy of stars that included Merle Oberon, Rita Hayworth, Ginger Rogers, Barbara Stanwyck, Edward G. Robinson, Charles Laughton, and Henry Fonda. The genre has retained its popularity to this day, especially in Europe.

In addition to the importance of the director and all-star casts to such enterprises, the more memorable creations of France's golden age of cinema depended also upon the contributions of other artists and craftsmen to the total impact of the films. The following sections discuss some of those who contributed the most lasting pleasure to the Saturday night filmgoers.

Screenwriters

In 1938, Antonin Artaud published *Le Théâtre et son double,* an essay which argues persuasively the need to break the tyranny of dialogue in the theater. Ironically, in the 1930s cinema it was the makers of dialogue, the scriptwriters, who, as the decade progressed, became instrumental in breaking the tyranny of the theater in the film industry. The best of them were also influential in bringing to the screen complex national problems and in reflecting the growing fissures in the social structure.

We have already examined numerous samples of their craft. Both Bernard Zimmer and Henri Jeanson worked on *Un Carnet de bal*. It was Zimmer who did the dialogue for *La Kermesse héroique*, skillfully injecting contemporary political concerns into language with a pleasantly archaic flavor. Later he teamed again with Feyder and with Jacques Viot on the screenplay of *Les Gens du voyage* (1937). It was Jeanson who made the creative adaptation of *Pépé-le-Moko* from a mediocre novel by Ashelbé, as well as that of *Le Drame de Shanghaï*. The most imposing figure among screenwriters from 1930 to 1950 was Charles Spaak, who worked a number of times with Feyder, Duvivier, Renoir, and Grémillon. His impressive list of credits, either as sole author or in collaboration, include *Le Grand jeu, Pension Mimosas, L'Homme du jour, La Belle équipe, La Fin du jour* (1938), *Gueule d'amour, La Petite Lise, Les Bas-fonds* (1936), and *La Grande illusion*. For his original scripts, he would begin not with an idea for a plot but with a particular location, a *milieu* which intrigued him and develop a story around it. The idea for *La Fin du jour* came to him when he and Duvivier were driving past a home for aging actors and he remarked to Duvivier that there was a film to be made there. The director agreed and together they worked out a narrative, from which Spaak did the dialogue. It was an audacious subject to undertake, since virtually all the characters were time-worn and *passé*, hardly a group to inspire great interest among the public. Although the film became a critical rather than commercial success, it remained Duvivier's favorite among his own pictures.

Perhaps the most inventive screenplay of the period was by Jacques Viot and Jacques Prévert, the script for *Le Jour se lève*. The narrative is unusual in that it makes extensive use of the flashback, a technique so innovative that it completely disoriented the first audiences, and a brief explanation of the plot had to be inserted at the beginning to help them navigate through repeated voyages forwards and backwards in time. It is the story of a man, François, who kills a rival, Valentin, then barricades himself in his room. There, he goes over in his mind the events that led up to the crime. The action shifts repeatedly from the present, as the police close in around him, to his memories, and then back again.

While Viot provided the inspiration for this novel disruption of linear narrative, it was Prévert, developing the dialogue from Viot's story line, who captured the climate of despair gripping France just prior to World War II. This feeling was particularly acute among the members of the working class, who had pinned such high hopes on the Front populaire only to see them dashed. The labor movement, so forceful in 1936, when widespread strikes threatened to bring the country to a standstill, responded with cynicism and apathy to a call for a general strike in 1938 in opposition to the Reynaud plan, which threatened to chip away many of the gains of the Matignon Accords. Many who had looked upon the Front populaire as the dawn of a new era were profoundly disillusioned by its all-too-rapid disintegration.

François is a worker who constantly wears the badge of his class, a cap, even when he is lying in bed about to make love to his mistress one Sunday morning. An unskilled laborer who has worked at a succession of brutalizing, low-paying, and unhealthy jobs, he is currently employed as a sandblaster. The conditions of his workplace are deplorable. The noise level is so high that it is necessary to scream to make oneself heard. The atmosphere is so noxious that flowers wilt and die in it after a few minutes, and François drinks milk, a traditional French folk remedy for poisons, in a vain attempt to counteract it. He and the other workers must dress in what look like bulky diving suits which strip them of their individual identities and allow them to descend daily into the figurative hell of jobs which are gradually killing them, as the sand inevitably finds its way into their lungs. It is a setting that makes a mockery of establishment clichés about the efficacy of work, as François is well aware: "In short, work is freedom . . . , and then health. It's true, this is a real healthy place here! . . . All day long we drink milk."[3]

Given his situation, François's hopes are suitably modest. He is in love with Francoise, an orphan like him. He would like to buy her a bicycle, so that at Easter they can ride off into the country and gather lilacs. He wants to marry her and have a family, but apparently even this is asking too much. When he first talks of marriage to her she is *visibly shocked, with a smile such as one has in the face of an absurdity.* Get married! *She looks at him.* How crazy you can be sometimes! . . . *She shrugs her shoulders.* Get married!" (17). She seems to consider it foolish for people in their position to have such expectations.

Any possibility of marriage is shattered when François shoots Valentin, who is about to taunt him with a description of how he seduced Françoise. François's crime, unlike that of Amedée Lange, is a strictly personal one and, although his fellow workers promise to stand by him if he surrenders to the police, it is clear that they would be able to do nothing for him. The feeling of solidarity and optimism of *Le Crime de Monsieur Lange* and, to a lesser extent, *La Belle équipe* is gone. So is the goodwill and good fellowship of the courtyard in the former and of the King of England Hotel and the joint restaurant venture in the latter. The crowd of onlookers that gathers below François's window contains hostile as well as sympathetic elements. The killing has cut François off from everyone else and he accepts his solitude, screaming at the crowd of gawkers to leave him in peace, that he is washed up, finished, and that there is nothing to look at anymore. As in the case of René in *La Vie est à nous*, a bourgeois lady simply assumes he is drunk: "How is it possible to get into such a state. . . . These workers, now, they think they can do anything. . . . So, they drink, they drink and then they commit crimes . . ." (36). François's outburst is cathartic, allowing him to accept his suicide with resignation. He shoots himself just as the police launch a final assault on his stronghold, dawn begins to break, and his alarm clock sounds its daily call to work.

It was original screenplays such as this that provided a viable alternative to the slavish transcription onto film of stage plays which dominated French production during the first half of the decade. Prévert's style was perfectly suited to the tragic narrative of a worker-hero. As in his poetry, Prévert brought to the screen a simplicity of language, dialogue such as might be heard in a bistro or on the street, but which was capable, like his verses, of conveying an atmosphere of lyric sadness. During the Nazi Occupation, Carné and Prévert continued to work together, making *Les Visiteurs du soir* (1942) and the exquisite *Les Enfants du paradis* (1944).

Composers

Ever since Camille Saint-Saens composed music for *L'Assassinat du Duc de Guise* (1908), musical scores have been written for films. In France in the 1920s, Honegger, Milhaud, and Auric were already active in the field and continued their work throughout the next decade. Although the coming of sound transformed film scores from a rarity into an element common to all movies, the composer's task was not always easy. Sometimes it was necessary to collaborate with a director with little or no musical sensitivity, or a producer with even less. Auric relates how a representative of the producer of Clair's *À nous la liberté*, for which he wrote the music, informed him that the easiest, that is, the most vulgar, score possible would be the best. And Honegger once did the title music for a film, only to be told that it was too beautiful and had been replaced by a popular tune. On the other hand, an intelligent director could use music most skillfully. In Pierre Chenal's *Crime et châtiment* (1935), by far the most interesting segment cinematographically comes at the beginning, when Raskolnikov (Pierre Blanchar) murders the pawnbroker. The sets, by Aimé Bazin, project something of the hallucinatory quality of German expressionism, complementing perfectly Blanchar's intensely haunted characterization, for which he won the prize for best actor at the Venice film festival in 1935. The sequence contains interesting camerawork, like the shot of Raskolnikov sneaking out of his lodgings in which we see only the silhouette of his top hat through the concierge's curtains. But the factor most instrumental in creating the scene's extreme tension is Honegger's score. The entire sequence contains almost no dialogue, only music which builds in intensity until the killing, after which, abruptly, it stops, giving way to natural sounds, such as the nerve-wracking rattling of keys in the corridor outside the door of the death room.

The composer who perhaps most fully seized the vast new potential of film music was Maurice Jaubert. Shunning the facile effects which quickly came to characterize the least imaginative background scores, Jaubert sought to create a music which would be a poetic extension of the image on the screen, which would make manifest its internal rhythm. He was interested in exploring the relationship between music and natural sounds and was well aware of the evocative value of silence. Duvivier said, "For Un Carnet de bal, it is Jaubert, the musician, who sometimes refused to compose music for a passage, realizing that it would have destroyed the equilibrium of the image, that it would have ruined rather than reinforced it."[4] Often his scores are quite brief; in L'Atalante, for example, there is only a total of about fifteen minutes of music. And in Zéro de conduite, music is virtually absent from the adult world, underlining the deadened state of all its members, with the exception of the child/adult Huguet.

Jaubert was a versatile craftsman, who could create an utterly accessible score for René Clair's Quatorze juillet which captured perfectly the atmosphere of local Parisien dances, a kind of music of the people much appreciated by Jacques Prévert. For the Prévert brothers' L'Affaire est dans le sac, he participated in the running joke about the fascist who throughout the film searches vainly for a beret with which to proclaim his political sympathies. He thinks he acquires one in a shop run by a gang of thieves. As he leaves the store, a blaring march begins which grows quickly louder. The man snaps into martial step to it and doffs his new hat to the military parade, suggested by the music but never seen. It is only then that he perceives that he has been sold a salopard's cap turned inside out! For the murder scene in Quai des brumes, Jaubert has his own composition, Ballades de Charles d'Orléans, played over the radio. As Jean kills Zabel, the soft, ethereal music provides a counterpoint to the brutal action, intensifying its savagery.

In Le Jour se lève, Jaubert's score contains comparatively little of melodic interest and no appreciable thematic development. The focus of the music lies elsewhere. Here it plays a key narrative role, providing, along with unusually long dissolves, passages of transition each time the scene shifts from present to past. It is precisely such moments, when film moves into areas beyond strict realism—the dormitory revolt in

Zéro de conduite, Christine's rose-colored reminiscences in *Un Carnet de bal*—that most intrigued Jaubert: "Here the music has something to say: its presence will warn the spectator that the style of the film is changing temporarily for dramatic reasons. All its power of suggestion will serve to intensify and prolong that impression of strangeness, of departure from photographic truth, which the director is seeking."[5] This is exactly how the two transitional themes—a limpid, nostalgic melody in the wind section and an oppressive rhythm in the percussion—function. The distinction between memory and actuality is further heightened by an almost complete absence of music during the remembered sequences themselves. By contrast, scenes set in the present have a musical background. As the narrative inexorably draws near its end, Jaubert uses a natural sound—as he had before with the train in *Zéro de conduite* and the barge motor in *L'Atalante*—as the rhythmic base of the music. Here it is François's heartbeat which provides the ominous pulsation in the drums that leads up to the suicide, breaking off abruptly when François fires a bullet into his heart. Tragically, Jaubert's career was also cut short by an enemy bullet in 1940 as he led his troops in battle just hours before France capitulated to the German invasion.

Set Designers

During the 1930s, sets in French films often achieved remarkable effects through a great economy of means. Lazare Meerson, the most influential designer of the decade, was especially skilled at this. For him decor had to be unobtrusive: "The decor accompanies the film, harmonises with it; it is from the decor that 'the atmosphere,' so valuable to the director and the actors, emanates."[6] His sets for *Sous les toits de Paris* provide an excellent illustration of this viewpoint. The film's entire action takes place in a small section of an old quarter of Paris. The characters are poor: Romanian immigrants, street singers, and petty crooks; their surroundings reflect their poverty, bordering on the squalid. Yet with cobblestone pavements, unimposing facades stripped of all unnecessary detail, and an archtypal local bistro, Meerson manages to infuse the movie with a delicate feeling of nostalgia, a poetry of the city and its common people. René Clair was well aware of the pivotal importance of Meerson's contribution: "Even in a naturalistic work, like *Under the Roofs of Paris*, sets provide an atmosphere that could never be obtained if I had shot in the streets. They compose reality, and that is my definition of art."[7]

Meerson also designed the factory in *À nous la liberté* which is so crucial in establishing the dehumanizing effect of industrial labor. The ultramodern facility, which seems large, is really a very small studio set 115 feet long. Meerson constructed the decor in perspective, arranging the assembly line workers according to height, placing the tallest in the foreground and children dressed as workers at the end. Its sterile functionalism contrasts markedly with the warmth of the decor in *Sous les toits de Paris*, whose characters, although impoverished, retain a strong sense of their basic worth within their little community. The factory, on the other hand, although materially productive, is a cold and harsh place which robs the workers of their satisfaction from work and individual dignity.

Meerson also collaborated with Feyder, creating a desert bistro in *Le Grand jeu* which reeks of absinthe, boredom, dust, and flies; but his most impressive achievement is unquestionably the set for *La Kermesse héroïque*. He began the project as usual by amassing a considerable amount of documentation on his subject, traveling to Flanders to take photographs, consulting books with relevant illustrations, and paintings in museums. From these he worked up sketches, relying on a blend of observation and imagination, constantly changing and modifying his plan right up to production time, adding little details even during the actual shooting, so that by the end of the filming the decor, built in the courtyard of the Tobis studios, had made incursions into the concierge's room and had spilled out into the street. The town with its peaceful canal and busy market, its opulent interiors which seem to come directly out of a Flemish painting, exudes an ambience of good and hearty eating and drinking, of the material well-being so characteristic of the Low Countries. In the distance, he placed models of roofs, bell towers, gables, and silhouettes of houses to create the illusion of the town stretching endlessly into the background. The set, which was kept intact until 1960, was so effective that it went far to lend substance and credibility to a plot that might otherwise have seemed dangerously slender. Meerson was such a diligent and demanding craftsman that his high standards proved disastrous to his health, bringing on death at the early age of thirty-eight.

Erich von Stroheim also did interesting work with decor in France in the 1930s. A legendary figure who had made such remarkable films as *Greed* (1923) in Hollywood in the 1920s, only to earn a reputation for extravagance that put him out of business as a director, he went on to fashion a second career for himself in Europe as an actor. His characterizations, like Hubert Kraal in *Macao, l'enfer du jeu* or Walter in *Les Disparus de Saint-Agil*, both men surrounded by an aura of mystery, often displayed a fascinating blend of tenderness and ruthlessness. Von Stroheim, who, like Françoise Rosay, always worked out the details of his own costuming, had the idea, in *La Grande illusion*, of placing von

Albert Préjean and Jany Holt in Pierre Chenal's L'Alibi.

Rauffenstein in a neck brace which reflects so eloquently his emotional, intellectual, and social rigidity. In Pierre Chenal's *L'Alibi* (1937), he plays an extravagant personnage, Winkler, a clairvoyant who is a night-club performer and a murderer. He dresses strikingly, in keeping with his calling, wearing a black cape/overcoat, a white straw hat, and white gloves when he spends the night with the heroine (innocently, like Kraal) to establish an alibi to cover his first killing. Von Stroheim also designed the decor for Winkler's fabulous studio, a large room decorated with stars, a skull, globes, a smoking urn, occult charts, and heavy carved wood furniture, a suitable den for a man of such diverse accomplishments. Von Stroheim continued his acting career for many years, appearing in both English and French speaking pictures. In 1950 he teamed up again with Gloria Swanson, the star of his ill-fated, final, unfinished Hollywood opus, *Queen Kelly* (1928), in Billy Wilder's acid portrait of Hollywood, *Sunset Boulevard*, in which they both play characters eerily close to their own personas.

Early in the decade, Meerson organized a group of young designers who learned their trade under his guidance, the most notable of which was Alexandre Trauner, who worked as his assistant on pictures by Clair and Feyder and later became a key member of the Carné/Prévert team, doing the decors for *Drôle de drame* (1937), *Quai des brumes, Hôtel du nord* (1938), *Le Jour se lève,* and collaborating on *Les Visiteurs du soir* and *Les Enfants du paradis.* His technique, modeled on Meerson's, involved the free and imaginative use of an immense documentation:

A true decor is not a copy; otherwise there would be no need of designers. To construct a true decor, the designer should perhaps draw more from his personal taste and memories than from a laborious documentation. It is his task to put in order all these elements to compose a true and credible image that the eye will accept as a reproduction of reality. It is his task to choose the accessories, the architectural styles, the materials which will give his work the desired character and climate.[8]

The set for *Le Jour se lève* provides a good illustration of this creative metamorphosis of reality. It is dominated by the six-story edifice at the top of which François has his room. Its tall facade reaches far above all the other buildings on the square in the working-class quarter of an industrialized provincial city, giving François's lodging the inaccessibility from the outside absolutely essential to the plot. Dwelling places so completely dissociated from the housing surrounding them are, to say the least, rare, but by unusual good fortune Trauner had come upon just such a one in Paris, while taking photographs in preparation for *Hôtel du nord,* located at the end of the Rue La Fayette, facing the canal Saint-Martin. With this as a basis, Trauner fashioned a building which, unlike the real one, is tapered toward the top, substantially increasing the feeling of François's extreme isolation. The soaring facade is illuminated during the night scenes by a street lamp with four bulbs, set far higher in the air than any found on real streets. Construction of the square was bankrolled by Dubonnet, four of whose *affiches* are plastered on one of the building's sides, an ironic touch given the readiness of both the police and the bourgeois lady to assume that François is a drunkard, a convenient way to avoid probing for and facing his real motives.

Within this remote edifice, François's room is even further cut off from the outside. The police first shoot out the windows of his garret and then the door. He only prevents them from bursting in by hastily pushing a huge Normandy wardrobe in front of the shattered door, virtually sealing off his chamber for the rest of the film, infusing it with a feeling of claustrophobia. To augment this constricted atmosphere, Carné insisted on a completely closed-in set with four immobile walls, all of which could be shown by the camera in a single movement. This presented no particular problem until the window and the door had been shot out with real bullets, rendering them unusable as entrances and exits. For the balance of the filming, so extreme was the closure that Carné, Gabin, and the crew with all its cumbersome equipment had to get in and out of the room through the ceiling by means of a ladder!

Inconvenient, but in Carné's estimation, well worth it: "Now I wanted an absolutely closed set, in order to give the impression of a man closed in, as it were, walled in this room where he was spending his final night, like a man condemned to death in his cell."[9]

It is tempting to see in François, scrunched into a corner of his cramped quarters, chainsmoking Gauloises, postponing yet at the same time awaiting the inevitable, an image of France at the moment the film was made, the time between Munich and the German invasion. "The motif of an 'obstructed path,' of blind alleys and blocked vistas, of faltering and stalemate, and of an increasingly desperate search for a way out, pervades the thinking of Frenchmen of all types and intellectual interests through nearly half a century following the outbreak of the First World War."[10] Seldom has the feeling of impasse been more acute than in those desolate days just before the fall of the Third Republic when France, closed in by hostile fascist states, hunkered down behind its Maginot Line, awaited the decade's inexorable conclusion. In this perspective, François's enclosed room may be taken as a microcosm of his deadlocked country's blocked options and imminent defeat.

6

Conclusion:
Influence of the Golden Age

MUCH WAS accomplished between the time that Al Jolson's rendition of "Sonny Boy." in *The Singing Fool* (1928) brought tears to the eyes of Jean-Paul Sartre, a hitherto staunch advocate of silent films, and the dark hour of the German invasion. The cinema transformed itself from an entertainment primarily for the lower class and for intellectuals into a mass media with distinctly bourgeois tastes. Symbolic of this shift, the movie house took its place beside legitimate theaters as the only locations of public entertainment where smoking, freely permitted before the coming of sound, was expressly forbidden. Film reviewing, sporadic at best in the silent era, became firmly established in the press.

Early in the decade, when bourgeois standards, exemplified by the *cinéma de boulevard*, reigned supreme, affronts to them were not taken lightly, as the swift suppression of *L'Âge d'or* and *Zéro de conduite* illustrates. Michel Simon's extraordinarily inventive portrayals of Boudu in Renoir's *Boudu sauvé des eaux* (1932) and of Père Jules in *L'Atalante* were not well received by either the public or the critics. Boudu, a bum rescued from suicide by a benevolent if fatuous bookstore owner, repays his benefactor by spitting on his rugs and in his rare volumes and by seducing his wife. At its premiere, the film provoked a riot. It is hard to say which element of misconduct was considered the most intolerable—perhaps Boudu eating sardines with his fingers—but incensed spectators ripped apart the theater seats and the movie was withdrawn after only three days. Michel Simon was stung by the vitriolic criticism and by the commercial failure of these two pictures. Although he went on to act in over forty films during the 1930s, his work, always competent and often excellent, became stripped of its madness, its eccentricity, and its anarchy.

Jean Gabin and Line Noro in a rare moment of tenderness in Julien Duvivier's Pépé le Moko. *Courtesy of Cinémathèque Française.*

Nonetheless, as the decade progressed, the grip of establishment norms gradually loosened. As the large production companies—Paramount, Gaumont, and Pathé—fell upon hard financial times, smaller producers, either through negligence or design, generated an atmosphere of greater creative freedom for filmmakers, and France found itself in the position to export a considerable number of movies that achieved prominent international stature. Significantly, in the latter half of the period, French films dominated the New York critics award for the best foreign film of the year. *La Kermesse héroïque* won the honor in 1936. *Mayerling*, the first French film to break out of the art film circuit to enjoy successful runs in the neighborhood American theaters, was chosen in 1937, *La Grande Illusion* in 1938, *Regain* in 1939, and *La Femme du boulanger* in 1940. So impressive was this output that, by the end of the 1930s, France was established without question as the art film center of the world.

The last feature film completed before the fall of France was Pierre Caron's *Ils étaient cinq permissionnaires* (1940). Others, like *Remorques* and Max Ophuls's *De Mayerling à Sarajevo* (1940), were interrupted and finished later, under less than ideal conditions. Another work in progress, René Clair's *Air pur,* was abandoned forever.

Although filmmaking was drastically curtailed during the Occupation, Carné and Grémillon managed to do some of their finest work during those difficult times: Grémillon made *Lumière d'été* (1942) and *Le Ciel est à vous* (1943), Carné *Les Visiteurs du soir* and *Les Enfants du paradis.* After the war, Grémillon once again experienced constant trouble in obtaining backing for his projects. And Carné seemed to find it impossible to equal the quality of his earlier films. Pagnol continued to produce movies set in the south of France, both during the Vichy government and after, notably *La Fille du puisatier* (1940) and *Manon des sources* (1952). Renoir, Duvivier, and Clair made movies in Hollywood during the war years and all went on to enjoy long and fruitful careers, although it may be argued with some justification that by the end of the 1930s their best work was behind them. Feyder died in 1948 and Benoit-Lévy, after fleeing France and the Occupation, never made another feature film.

A number of younger directors, who served their apprenticeship in the 1930s, came into their own in the succeeding two decades: Jacques Becker, who worked as an assistant to Renoir; Yves Allégret, who was an assistant to his brother Marc, to Renoir and others; Henri-Georges Clouzot and Claude Auntant-Lara, to name but a few. So many of the major directors of the 1940s and 1950s learned their trade in the 1930s that it is not surprising that much of their work looks back in form and substance to that decade.

Thus, there is a certain irony in the way in which the Nouvelle Vague directors rebelled against what they felt to be the uninspired predictability of the postwar cinema. Skilled technicians from the 1930s like Christian-Jaque and Jean Delannoy, who were still practicing their craft, figured prominently on Jean-Luc Godard's blacklist. Yet the Nouvelle Vague also reached back to the Golden Age for inspiration. Truffaut once remarked, "We are all the children of *Toni*," and his first feature, *Les Quatre cent coups* (1959), contains strong links to Vigo's films, both in spirit and in actual references, such as Antoine's final dash to the sea, so reminiscent of Jean's futile run seaward in *L'Atalante*. More recently, Truffaut has used Maurice Jaubert's 1930s music to construct film scores for *L'Histoire d'Adèle H.*, *L'Argent de poche* (*Small Change*, 1976), *L'Homme qui aimait les femmes* (1977), and *La Chambre verte* (1978). And Godard, in *À bout de souffle* (1959), takes up again the mythical figure embodied so often in the 1930s by Gabin. His hero, played with such casual perfection by Jean-Paul Belmondo, is a car thief and murderer, a dropout and an outsider. He falls in love with a vendor of the *Herald Tribune*, whom he tries to convince to run away with him. But, like Jean in *Quai des brumes*, he is gunned down in the street, his love leading him not to a new life but to death. For Godard, the Gabin myth receives its final send-up in Pierrot's dynamite suicide in *Pierrot le fou* (1966).

Immediately after World War II, two countries which made only modest contributions to the field of feature films in the 1930s, Italy and England, began to turn out excellent work. Italian neo-realism in particular, with its accent on improvisation, nonprofessional actors, shooting in the streets, and on works in which the message was all-important, revolutionized filmmaking, sounding the death knell for the formality of the theatrical movie. In this respect, it is interesting to note that one of the precursors of this new wave of realism was none other than the original exponent of canned theater, Marcel Pagnol, whose loving use of Provençal exteriors paved the way for the more daring experiments of the Italians. The other French forerunner was Renoir, especially in *Toni* (1935), a movie also made in the south of France and facilitated by Pagnol, shot mostly with exteriors in the countryside around Martigues. Its plot, related without ornamentation, is based on a *fait divers*, a murder involving the Italian and Spanish laborers who work in the area. Another link with Renoir is provided by Luchino Visconti, who worked with Renoir on *Une partie de campagne* (1936) and Carl Koch's *La Tosca* (1940). It was Visconti's *Ossessione* (1942), an adaptation of James Cain's *The Postman Always Rings Twice*, which marks the beginning of the neo-realist movement. French influence is equally apparent when certain of the Italian directors began to move away from strict realism. The element of fantasy in de Sica's *Miracle in Milan* (1950), the lighter treatment of themes such as poverty and exploitation, so grindingly presented in *The Bicycle Thief* (1948), owes much to the free play of creative imagination in René Clair's *Le Million* and *À nous la liberté*.

Similarly, the influence of the 1930s French cinema on postwar English films is significant and may be conveniently illustrated by two examples. *Kind Hearts and Coronets* by Robert Hamer, which epitomizes a kind of quintessential British humor at its best, owes its narrative structure to the innovations of Sacha Guitry. The film, like *Le Roman d'un tricheur*, is narrated voice-over by the hero, a very deadly *tricheur* who ascends into the aristocracy by murdering everyone in his family who stands in his way, and who is, like Guitry's central character, writing his memoirs. And Carol Reed's *Odd Man Out* (1947) offers an Irish/English variant of the Gabin myth. The hero, played by James Mason, is a revolutionary and a criminal hunted by the police, doomed to failure and a violent end. He, too, cannot be saved by love and his death is a close reenactment of the final scene in *Pépé-le-Moko*. Like Pépé, he is trapped against the barrier of an iron fence. As the boat which promised him escape pulls away from the wharf, he is killed in a barrage of police fire.

The influence of the golden age of French cinema continues to be strong. Before embarking on his career as a filmmaker, Ingmar Bergman is reputed to have made an exhaustive study of Duvivier's best movies frame by frame. Before beginning work on *If* (1968), Lindsay Anderson made a point of rereading the screenplay of *Zéro de conduite*, and his film is clearly infused with Vigo's revolutionary spirit. Even so seemingly modern a picture as Bertolucci's *Last Tango in Paris* (1972) is full of echoes of the 1930s. Although shot in color, its soft focus recalls Carné's in *Le Jour se lève*. Jeanne, the elusive fiancée chased by Tom, is like a more modern, freer version of Juliette, the runaway bride in *L'Atalante*. But the strongest similarity lies in the character of Paul. As played by Brando, he has a great deal of Michel Simon's antibourgeois madness and anarchy, as when he moons the stiff and lacquered tango dancers, themselves throwbacks to the 1930s. Perhaps even more, he is a contemporary embodiment of the Gabin myth, a former political activist, an outcast of society, whose life has closed in on him like François's in *Le Jour se lève*. Like Gabin's characters, Paul is full of frustration and desperation which find an outlet in his sexual assaults on Jeanne. But these only afford temporary relief at best and his life remains confined, like François's, to the apartment where they meet and to the seedy hotel inhabited by his dead wife's lover. Paul, like so many of Gabin's heroes and their modern brothers, seems destined to failure and to violent death. For Paul, even love has become grotesque, and it is fitting that in his case the trigger is pulled by the very woman he so desperately clings to.

These are some of the more prominent examples illustrating the breadth of the impact which the French cinema of the 1930s continues to exert, which indicate as well its pivotal importance in the historical and aesthetic development of filmmaking.

Notes and References

Chapter One

1. Noël Burch, *Marcel L'Herbier* (Paris: Seghers, 1973), p. 28.

Chapter Two

1. Claude Arnulf, Jacques Fieschi, and Bernard Minoret, "Entretien avec Marcel L'Herbier," *Cinématographe*, no. 40 (n.d.), p. 41.
2. Ibid., p. 41.
3. Robert Daudelin, "Mon gosse de père (1930)," *Cinéma de France 1930–39; La Cinémathèque Québécoise*, June 1976, p. 11.
4. Ivor Winters, "An Interview with Alberto Cavalcanti," *Screen* 13, no. 2 (Summer 1972), p. 36.
5. Luis Buñuel, "L'Âge d'or," in *L'Avant-Scène*, nos. 27-28 (December 1962), p. 41.
6. Quoted in Mireille Latil Le Dantic, "Jean Grémillon, Le réalisme et le tragique," *Cinématographe*, no. 40 (October 1978), p. 43.
7. Quoted in Francis Courtade, *Les Malédictions du cinéma français* (Paris, 1978), p. 54.
8. Ibid., p. 54.
9. Jean Renoir, "La Chienne," *L'Avant-Scène*, no. 162 (October 1975), p. 8. All further page references in the text are to this published screenplay.
10. Georges Sadoul, *Dictionnaire des films* (Paris: Seuil, 1978), p. 154.
11. René Clair, *Cinéma d'hier, cinéma d'aujourd'hui* (Paris, 1970), p. 96.
12. Ibid., p. 207.
13. Claude Beylie and Guy Braucourt, "Entretien avec Marcel Pagnol," *Cinéma 69*, no. 134 (March 1969), p. 44.
14. Alexandre Arnoux, *Du muet au parlant* (Paris: La Nouvelle Edition, 1946), pp. 131–32.
15. Quoted in Jacques Siclier, "Guitry," in *Anthologie du cinéma* II (Paris: L'Avant-Scène, 1967), 2:127.

Chapter Three

1. Charles Baudelaire, *Les Fleurs du mal et autres poèmes* (Paris: Gallimard, 1964), p. 151.
2. Ibid.
3. Gordon Wright, *France in Modern Times* (Chicago, 1974), p. 352.
4. René Maran, *Batouala*, trans. Barbara Beck and Alexandre Mboukou (Greenwich, Conn.: Fawcett Books, 1974), p. 86.
5. Quoted in Pierre Boulanger, *Le Cinéma colonial* (Paris, 1975), p. 115.
6. Jean Benoit-Lévy, *Les Grandes missions du cinéma* (Montreal, 1945), p. 318.
7. Interview with Marie Epstein, 21 July 1979; a subsequent reference to her views is also drawn from this interview.
8. Boulanger, *Le Cinéma colonial*, p. 116.
9. Isaac Yetiv, *Le Thème de l'alienation dans le roman Maghrébin de l'expression française de 1952 à 1956* (Sherbrooke, Quebec: University of Sherbrooke Press, 1972), p. 22.
10. Benoit-Lévy, *Les Grandes missions*, p. 315.
11. Sadoul, *Dictionnaire des films*, p. 131.
12. Jacques Feyder and Françoise Rosay, *Le Cinéma, notre metier* (Geneva, 1946), p. 44.
13. Jacques Feyder, Charles Spaak, and Bernard Zimmer, "La Kermesse héroïque," *L'Avant-Scène*, no. 26 (May 1963), p. 18. All further quotations from the film are from this edition.
14. Baudelaire, *Les Fleurs*, p. 154.
15. Quoted in Pierre Galante, *Malraux* (Paris: Plon, 1971), p. 161.
16. Quoted in Denis Marion, *André Malraux* (Paris, 1970), p. 99.

Chapter Four

1. Jean-Pierre Jeancolas, "Les Pésanteurs sociologiques du cinéma français 1930–1939," *Cinéma de France 1930–1939: La Cinémathèque Québécoise,* June 1976, p. 3.
2. Simone de Beauvoir, *The Prime of Life*, trans. Peter Green (New York, 1973), p. 160.
3. Henri Noguères, *La Vie quotidienne au temps du Front populaire 1935–1938* (Paris, 1977), p. 109.
4. Ibid., p. 105.
5. Quoted in Henri Agel, *Jean Grémillon* (Paris: Seghers, 1969) p. 48.
6. Ibid., p. 54.
7. Quoted in Jean-Patrick Lebel, *"Zéro de conduite," IDHEC Fiche filmographique*, no. 181 (n.d.), p. 1.
8. Benoit-Lévy, *Les Grandes missions*, p. 222.
9. Ibid., p. 237.
10. Ibid., pp. 50–52.
11. See Noguères, *La Vie*, pp. 50–52.
12. Quoted in René Prédal, *La Societé française à travers le cinéma* (Paris, 1972), p. 228.

13. Ibid., p. 229.
14. De Beauvoir, *Prime of Life*, p. 362.
15. Quoted in Raymond Chirat, "Julien Duvivier," in *Premier Plan* (Lyon: Serdoc, 1968), p. 105.
16. De Beauvoir, *Prime of Life*, p. 362.
17. Quoted in Sadoul, *Dictionnaire des films*, p. 215.
18. Quoted in Alexander Sesonske, *Jean Renoir: The French Films, 1924–1939* (Cambridge, Mass., 1980), p. 382.
19. Prédal, *La Societé*, p. 159.
20. Ibid., p. 159.
21. Janet Flanner, *Paris Was Yesterday*, ed. Irving Drutman (New York, 1972), p. 196.
22. Alfred Cobban, *A History of Modern France* (Baltimore: Penguin, 1965), 3:144.

Chapter Five

1. Marcel Oms, "Le Temps du 'cinoche,'" *Les Cahiers de la Cinémathèque*, nos. 23–24 (December 1977), p. 10.
2. Flanner, *Paris Was Yesterday*, pp. 169–70.
3. Jacques Prévert and Jacques Viot, *"Le Jour se lève,"* *L'Avant-Scène du cinéma*, no. 53 (1965), p. 16. All further quotations from the film are taken from this text.
4. Quoted in François Porcile, *Maurice Jaubert: musicien populaire ou maudit?* (Paris: Editeurs français réunis, 1971), p. 217.
5. Maurice Jaubert, "Music on the Screen," in *Footnotes to the Film*, ed. Charles Davy (London, 1937), p. 109.
6. Quoted in Léon Barsacq, *Le Décor du film* (Paris: Seghers, 1970), p. 199.
7. Charles T. Samuels, *Encountering Directors* (New York: Putnam, 1972), p. 84.
8. Barsacq, *Le Décor*, p. 199.
9. Marcel Carné, *La Vie à belles dents* (Paris, 1975), p. 148.
10. H. Stuart Hughes, *The Obstructed Path: French Social Thought in the Years of Desperation 1930–1960* (New York: Harper and Row, 1966), p. 1.

Selected Bibliography

Film Scripts

L'Âge d'or. L'Avant-Scène du cinéma, nos. 27–28 (December 1962). Also contains *Un chien andalou* and Buñuel's *L'Ange exterminateur.*

À nous la liberté. L'Avant-Scène du cinéma, no. 86 (November 1968). Published in English: René Clair, *À Nous la Liberté and Entr'acte* (New York: Simon and Schuster, 1971).

La Chienne. L'Avant-Scène du cinéma, no. 162 (October 1975).

La Grande illusion. L'Avant-Scène du cinéma, no. 21 (December 1962). Published in English: Jean Renoir, *Grande Illusion,* trans. Marianne Alexander and Andrew Sinclair (New York: Simon & Schuster, 1968).

Le Jour se lève. L'Avant-Scène du cinéma, no. 53 (n.d.). Published in English: Marcel Carné and Jacques Prévert, *Le Jour se lève,* trans. Dinah Brooke and Nicola Hayden (New York: Simon & Schuster, 1970).

La Kermesse héroïque. L'Avant-Scène du cinéma, no. 26 (December 1963).

La Règle du jeu. L'Avant-Scène du cinéma, no. 52 (October 1965). Published in English: Jean Renoir, *The Rules of the Game,* trans. John McGrath and Maureen Teitelbaum (New York: Simon & Schuster, 1970).

Zéro de conduite. L'Avant-Scène du cinéma, no. 21 (December 1962). Also contains Renoir's *Une partie de campagne.*

Secondary Sources

Andrew, Dudley. "Sound in France: The Origins of a Native School," *Yale French Studies,* no. 60 (1980), pp. 94–114. A succinct and intelligent overview of the transition to sound with special focus on *La Petite Lise.*

Anthologie du cinéma. Vol. 11. Paris: L'Avant-Scène, 1967. Contains chapters on Guitry, Feyder, Vigo, and Grémillon.

Beauvoir, Simone de. *The Prime of Life,* translated by Peter Green. New York: Lancer Books, 1973. The volume of her autobiography covering the decade of the 1930s.

Benoit-Lévy, Jean. *Les Grandes missions du cinéma.* Montreal: Parizeau, 1945. A presentation of his ideas on film with particular stress on its educational potential.

146

Beylie, Claude. *Marcel Pagnol.* Paris: Seghers, 1975. The best, most thorough work to date on Pagnol the filmmaker, illuminated by Beylie's personal contact with Pagnol.

Boulanger, Pierre. *Le Cinéma colonial.* Paris: Seghers, 1975. A vast and useful account of colonialist films from the silent era to the dissolution of the Empire.

Bounoure, Gaston. *Remorques,* Typescript fiche filmographique, no. 72. Paris: IDHEC, n.d. A detailed analysis of the film, one of the best in IDHEC's collection.

Brunius, Jacques-B. *En marge du cinéma français.* Paris: Arcanes, 1954. Contains information on the period of the 1930s from a member of "Groupe Octobre" who was, at the time, actively involved in films, both behind and before the camera.

Carné, Marcel. *La Vie à belles dents.* Paris: Jean-Pierre Olliver, 1975. The memoirs of the *cinéaste,* both as assistant to Feyder and as director.

Chirat, Raymond. *Catalogue des films français de long métrage—Films sonores de fiction, 1929–1939.* Brussels: Cinémathèque royale de Belgique, 1975. An exhaustive, authoritative, indispensable filmography of over 1,300 feature films from the period, to be followed by similar one for the 1940s.

"Le Cinéma du sam'di soir." *Les Cahiers de la cinémathèque,* nos. 23–24 (Christmas 1977). Excellent special issue on the 1930s French cinema by the Cinémathèque de Toulouse, which has undertaken a reevaluation of the period. Further articles on the subject are promised.

Cinéma de France. 1929–1939, edited by Robert Daudelin. Montreal: La Cinémathèque Québécoise, 1976. Brochure for a retrospective of 1930s French film, containing useful program notes on individual films. Also contains a reprint of an excellent article, "Les Pésanteurs sociologiques du cinéma français 1930–1939," by Jean-Pierre Jeancolas.

Clair, René. *Cinéma d'hier, cinéma d'aujourd'hui.* Paris: Gallimard, 1970. Invaluable reminiscences on his career, particularly on his adaption to sound.

Courtade, Francis. *Les Malédictions du cinéma français.* Paris: Alain Moreau, 1978. An authoritative, detailed, and invaluable examination of the problems which have beset the French film industry from the beginning of the sound era to the present.

Daniel, Joseph. *Guerre et cinéma—Grandes illusions et petits soldats.* Paris: Armand Colin, 1972. A thorough and thoughtful analysis of French war movies from the silents through the 1960s.

"Du muet au parlant." *Cinématographe,* no. 47 (May 1979), pp. 1–27. Special issue on the coming of sound to America and Europe.

Dupont, Jacques. *Pépé le Moko,* Fiche filmographique, no. 101. Paris: IDHEC, n.d. A succinct study of the film.

Feyder, Jacques, and Rosay, Françoise. *Le Cinéma notre métier,* Geneva: Skira, 1944. The memoirs of the husband and wife who played a vital role in the rebirth of French cinema in the 1930s. Useful information on the making of Feyder's films.

Fescourt, Henri. *La Foi et les montagnes.* Paris: Publications Photo-Cinéma Paul Montel, 1959. The memoirs of a director caught in the difficult transition to sound, which capture very well the chaotic flavor of the critical years.

Fischer, Lucy. "René Clair, *Le Million* and the Coming of Sound," *Cinema Journal* 16, no. 2 (Spring 1977):34–50. A perceptive analysis of Clair's use of sound in the film.

Flanner, Janet. *Paris Was Yesterday: 1925–1939.* New York: Viking 1972. A compilation of her letters from Paris to the *New Yorker* which provide a good feeling for the spirit of the 1930s and much useful information on the decade as well.

Les Français et leur cinéma—1930–1939. Paris: Eric Losfeld, 1973. Brochure which accompanied a retrospective of 1930s French film given at Maison de Culture de Créteil with the participation of the Cinémathèque de Toulouse. The Jeancolas article, "Les Pésanteurs sociologiques du cinéma français 1930–1939," first appeared here.

Gomery, Douglas. "Economic Struggle and Hollywood Imperialism: Europe Converts to Sound," *Yale French Studies,* no. 60 (1980), pp. 80–93. Useful information on the business aspects of the changeover to sound.

Gorbman, Claudia. "Clair's Sound Hierarchy and the Creation of Auditory Space," *Purdue Film Studies Annual,* 1976, pp. 113–23. An excellent analysis of Clair's innovative use of sound in *Sous les toits de Paris.*

Insdorf, Annette. "Maurice Jaubert and Francois Truffaut: Musical continuities from *L'Atalante* to *L'Histoire d'Adèle H.*" *Yale French Studies,* no. 60 (1980), pp. 204–18. Elucidates an important aspect of the continuing influence of the 1930s cinema on Truffaut.

Jaubert, Maurice. "Music on the Screen," In *Footnotes to the Film,* edited by Charles Davy. London: Lovat and Dickson, 1937, pp. 101–15. Jaubert's theory of the proper function of film music.

"Jean Vigo." *études cinématographiques,* nos. 51–52 (1966). A special issue with penetrating articles on varied aspects of Vigo's work.

Krier, J. *Marius.* Typescript fiche filmographique, no. 23, Paris: IDHEC, n.d. Analysis of the film in considerable detail.

Le Dantec, Mireille Latil. "Jean Grémillon, Le Réalisme et le tragique," *Cinématographe,* nos. 40–41 (October–November 1978), pp. 43–50, 35–44. A perceptive account of Grémillon's long, often frustrating career with brief but insightful reference to the individual films.

Marie, Michel. "The Poacher's Aged Mother: On Speech in *La Chienne* by Jean Renoir," *Yale French Studies* 60 (1980):219–32. An excellent analysis of Renoir's use of sound in the film.

Marion, Dennis. *André Malraux.* Paris: Seghers, 1970. A highly useful account of the filming of *L'Espoir* by one of the direct participants in its making.

Noguères, Henri. *La Vie quotidienne en France au temps du Front populaire.* Paris: Hachette, 1977. A valuable chronicle of the rise and fall of the Front populaire by an active and sympathetic participant.

Panigel, Armand. *Histoire du cinéma français par ceux qui l'ont fait.* A series of broadcasts on the Télévision Française (1974–75). Covers the period from the birth of sound to that of the Nouvelle Vague, combining interviews with actors and directors such as Clair, Carné, Michel Simon, and Christian-Jaque with numerous clips from films. Contains a wealth of information and is available on video cassette from FACSEA.

Porcile, François. *Maurice Jaubert: Musicien populaire ou maudit?* Paris: Editeurs Français réunis, 1971. A thorough and valuable discussion of Jaubert's concert and film works.

Prédal, René. *La Société française à travers le cinéma.* Paris: Armand Colin, 1972. A very useful compendium, comprised for the 1930s period mostly of excerpts from film scripts and critical reviews from the era.

Sesonke, Alexandre. *Jean Renoir: The French Films, 1924–1939.* Cambridge, Mass.: Harvard University Press, 1980. A detailed analysis of most of the films which benefits from a close personal relationship with Renoir during his later years in California.

Salles Gomes, P. E. *Jean Vigo.* Paris: Editions du Seuil, 1957. Also available in English (Berkeley: University of California Press, 1971). Provides a wealth of biographical material and detailed information on the circumstances under which the films were made. An essential book on Vigo.

Strebel, Elizabeth Grottle. "Renoir and the Popular Front," *Sight and Sound* 49 (Winter 1979–80):36–41. Perceptive analysis of *Le Crime de Monsieur Lange* and *La Marseillaise* against the backdrop of the Front populaire.

Travelling. no. 47 (Autumn 1976), pp. 3–43. A special issue on Christian-Jaque which traces his long career, with valuable information on his early apprenticeship at Paramount.

Wright, Gordon. *France in Modern Times,* 2d ed. Chicago: Rand McNally, 1974. Contains an accessible account of the decade, as well as of the years preceding and following it.

Filmography

A chronological listing of those major films easily available in the United States.

SOUS LES TOITS DE PARIS (Société des Films Sonores Tobis, 1930)
Director: René Clair
Assistant Directors: Georges Lacombe, Marcel Carné, Jacques Houssin
Screenplay: René Clair
Cinematographer: Georges Périnal, Georges Raulet
Set Decoration: Lazare Meerson
Costumes: René Hubert
Music: Armand Bernard, Raoul Moretti (lyrics), René Nazelles, André Gailhard
Sound: Hermann Storr, W. Morhenn
Editor: René Le Hénaff
Cast: Pola Illery (Pola), Albert Préjean (Albert), Gaston Modot (Fred), Edmond de Gréville (Louis)
Running time: 80 minutes
Premiere: 2 January 1930, Moulin Rouge, Paris
16mm. Rental: Audio Brandon, Images, Corinth, Kit Parker, Budget, Select, Westcoast, Em Gee Film Library. Only the Audio Brandon print has the original opening of people taking cover in a rain shower.

L'ÂGE D'OR (1930)
Director: Luis Buñuel
Producer: Vicomte de Noailles
Assistant Directors: Jacques-Bernard Brunius, Claude Heymann
Screenplay: Luis Buñuel, Salvatore Dali
Cinematographer: Albert Duverger
Set Decoration: Pierre Schildknecht
Music: Mendelson, Mozart, Beethoven, Debussy, Wagner, Georges Van Parys
Sound: Peter-Paul Brauer
Editor: Luis Buñuel
Cast: Gaston Modot, Pierre Prévert, Max Ernst, Lya Lys, Germaine Noizet
Running time: 62 minutes
Premiere: 3 December 1930, Studio 28, Paris
16mm. Rental: Corinth, Em Gee Film Library

LE MILLION (Société des Films Sonores Tobis, 1931)
Director: René Clair
Assistant Director: Georges Lacombe
Screenplay: René Clair, from Georges Berr and Marcel Guillemaud's play, *Le Million*
Cinematographer: Georges Périnal, Georges Raulet
Set Decoration: Lazare Meerson
Costumes: Georges K. Benda
Music: Armand Bernard, Georges Van Parys, Philippe Parès
Sound: Hermann Storr
Editor: René Le Hénaff
Cast: Annabella (Béatrice), Wanda Gréville (Wanda), Odette Talazac (the soprano), René Lefèvre (Michel), Paul Ollivier (le père la Tulipe), Louis Allibert (Prosper), Constantin Stroesco (Sopranelli)
Running time: 91 minutes
Premiere: 15 April 1931, Les Miracles Théâtre, Paris
16mm. Rental: Audio Brandon, Corinth, Kit Parker, Images, Budget, Museum of Modern Art, Classic Film Museum, Em Gee Film Library, Ivy, Select, Video Communications, Westcoast

LA CHIENNE (Etablissements Braunberger-Richebé, 1931)
Director: Jean Renoir
Producers: Pierre Braunberger, Robert Richebé
Assistant Directors: Pierre Prévert, Claude Heymann, Pierre Schwab, Yves Allégret
Screenplay: Jean Renoir, André Girard, from Georges de la Fouchardière's novel, *La Chienne* (1930)
Cinematographer: Theodore Sparkhul, Roger Hubert
Set Decoration: Gabriel Scognamillo
Sound: Marcel Courmes, Joseph de Bretagne, Denise Batcheff
Editor: Marguerite Renoir, Jean Renoir
Cast: Michel Simon (Maurice Legrand), Janie Marèze (Lulu), Georges Flamant (Dédé), Magdeleine Bérubet (Adèle Legrand), Gaillard (Alexis Godard)
Running time: 90 minutes
Premiere: 19 November 1931, Colisée, Paris
16mm. Rental: Audio Brandon

MARIUS (Paramount, 1931)
Director: Alexander Korda
Producer: Robert T. Kane
Screenplay: Marcel Pagnol, from his play, *Marius* (1929); Pagnol also supervised the filming
Cinematographer: Ted Pahle
Set Decoration: Alfred Junge, Zoltan Korda
Music: Francis Gorman
Editor: Roger Spiri-Mercanton
Cast: Raimu (César), Pierre Fresnay (Marius), Orane Demazis (Fanny), Fer-

nand Charpin (Panisse), Alida Rouffe (Honorine)
Running time: 125 minutes
Premiere: October 1931, salle Paramount, Paris
16mm. Rental: Images, Kit Parker, Budget

POIL DE CAROTTE (Film d'Art, 1932)
Director: Julien Duvivier
Producer: Vandal, Dulac
Assistant Directors: Ary Sadoul, Gilbert de Knyff
Screenplay: Julien Duvivier, from Jules Renard's play, *Poil de Carotte* (1900), and *La Bigote* (1910)
Cinematographer: Armand Thirard, Moniot
Set Decoration: Lucien Aguettand, Carré
Music: Alexandre Tansman
Sound: Roger Handjian, Lucy Sarrazin
Editor: Marthe Poncin, Jean Feyte
Cast: Robert Lynen (François—Poil de Carotte), Harry Baur (M. Lepic), Catherine Fontenay (Mme Lepic), Christiane Dor (Annette), Louis Gauthier (the stepfather)
Running time: 85 minutes
16mm. Rental: Kit Parker, Budget, Em Gee Film Library

BOUDU SAUVE DES EAUX (Société Sirius, 1932; American title, Boudu Saved from Drowning)
Director: Jean Renoir
Producer: Michel Simon
Assistant Directors: Jacques Becker, Georges Darnoux
Screenplay: Jean Renoir, Albert Valentin, from René Fauchois's play, *Boudu sauvé des eaux* (1919)
Cinematographers: Marcel Lucien, Georges Asselin
Set Decoration: Hugues Laurent, Jean Castanier
Music: Raphael, Johann Strauss
Sound: Igor B. Kalinowski
Editor: Suzanne de Troye, Marguerite Renoir
Cast: Michel Simon (Boudu), Charles Granval (M. Lestingois), Marcelle Hainia (Mme Lestingois), Séverine Lerczinska (Anne-Marie), Jean Dasté (the student), Jean Gehret (Vigour), Jacques Becker (the poet)
Running time: 89 minutes
Premiere: 11 November 1932, Colisée, Paris
16mm. Rental: Audio Brandon, Corinth, Kit Parker, Budget, Em Gee Film Library

FANNY (Les Films Marcel Pagnol, Etablissements Braunberger, Richebé, 1932)
Director: Marc Allégret
Producer: Roger Richebé
Assistant Directors: Pierre Prévert, Yves Allégret, Eli Lotar
Screenplay: Marcel Pagnol, from his play, *Fanny* (1931); Pagnol also supervised the filming

Cinematographers: Nicolas Toporkoff, Roger Huber, Georges Benoit, André Dantan. Coutelen, Roger Forster
Set Decoration: Gabriel Scognamillo
Music: Vincent Scotto, Georges Sellers (arrangements)
Sound: W. Bell
Editor: Jean Mamy
Cast: Orane Demaziz (Fanny), Raimu (César), Alida Rouffe (Honorine), Fernand Charpin (Panisse), Pierre Fresnay (Marius)
Running time: 122 minutes
Premiere: October 1932, Marigny, Paris
16mm. Rental: Images, Budget, Kit Parker

ZERO DE CONDUITE (Argui-Films, 1933)
Director: Jean Vigo
Producer: Jacques-Louis Nounez
Assistant Directors: Albert Riéra, Henri Storck, Pierre Merle
Screenplay: Jean Vigo
Cinematographer: Boris Kaufman
Set Decoration: Jean Vigo, Boris Kaufman, Henri Storck
Music: Maurice Jaubert, Charles Goldblatt (songs)
Sound: Royne, Bocquel
Editor: Jean Vigo
Cast: Louis Lefèvre (Caussat), Gilbert Pluchon (Colin), Gérard de Bédarieux (Tabard), Constantin Goldstein-Kehler (Bruel), Jean Dasté (Huguet), Robert Le Flon (M. Parrain or Dry Fart), Delphin (the principal), Blanchar (the assistant principal or Gas Snout), Léon Larive (the chemistry teacher)
Running time: 44 minutes
Premiere: 7 April 1933, Cinéma Artistic, Paris, then censored until November 1945, Le Pantheon, Paris. In the meantime, it was shown only in film clubs.
16mm. Rental: Audio Brandon, Images, Kit Parker, Budget, Classic Film Museum, Em Gee Film Library, Institutional Cinema, Ivy

LA MATERNELLE (Photosonor, 1933)
Directors: Marie Epstein and Jean Benoit-Lévy
Producer: Beau
Screenplay: Marie Epstein and Jean Benoit-Lévy, from Leon Frapié's novel
Cinematographer: Georges Asselin
Set Decoration: Robert Bassi
Music: Edouard Flament
Sound: Jean Dubuis
Cast: Madeleine Renaud (Rose), Paulette Elambert (Marie Coeuret), Mady Berry (Mme Paulin), Henri Debain (Doctor Libois), Alice Tissot (the directrice)
Running time: 100 minutes
Premiere: April 1933, Studio, Paris
16mm. Rental: Museum of Modern Art. A shot of Marie, nude and being dried off, and shots of children seated on latrines, have been edited out of this print.

LE GRAND JEU (Les Films de France, 1933)
Director: Jacques Feyder

Assistant Directors: Marcel Carné, Henri Chomette
Screenplay: Charles Spaak, Jacques Feyder
Cinematographer: Harry Stradling, Maurice Forster
Set Decoration: Lazare Meerson
Music: Hanns Eisler
Editor: Jacques Brillouin
Cast: Marie Bell (Florence and Irma), Pierre Richard-Willm (Pierre), Françoise Rosay (Blanche), Charles Vanel (Clément), Georges Pitoëff (Nicolas)
Running time: 115 minutes
Premiere: 27 April 1934, Marignan, Paris
16mm. Rental: French American Cultural Services and Educational Aid (FACSEA)

L'ATALANTE (Gaumont-Franco-Film-Aubert, 1934)
Director: Jean Vigo
Producer: Jacques-Louis Nounez
Assistant Directors: Albert Riéra, Pierre Merle
Screenplay: Jean Vigo, Albert Riéra, Jean Guinée
Cinematographer: Boris Kaufman
Set Decoration: Francis Jourdain
Music: Maurice Jaubert
Editor: Louis Chavance
Cast: Michel Simon (Père Jules), Jean Dasté (Jean), Dita Parlo (Juliette), Gilles Margaritis (the peddler)
Running time: 89 minutes
Premiere: 13 September 1934, Colisée, Paris, as *Le Chaland qui passe*. Restored insofar as possible to its original form and presented with its original title on 30 October 1940, Studio des Ursulines, Paris
16mm. Rental: Audio Brandon, Images, Kit Parker, Budget, Classic Film Museum, Em Gee Film Library, Ivy, Select, Westcoast

LA KERMESSE HEROÏQUE (Société des Films Sonores Tobis, 1935; American title, Carnival in Flanders)
Director: Jacques Feyder
Assistant Director: Marcel Carné
Screenplay: Jacques Feyder, Charles Spaak, Bernard Zimmer (dialogue), from Charles Spaak's short story
Cinematographers: Harry Stradling, Louis Page, André Thomas
Set Decoration: Lazare Meerson, Alexandre Trauner, Georges Wakhevitch
Costumes: Georges K. Benda
Music: Louis Beydts
Sound: Hermann Storr
Editor: Jacques Brillouin
Cast: Françoise Rosay (Cornelia), Jean Murat (the duke), André Alerme (the burgomaster), Micheline Cheirel (Siska), Bernard Lancret (Jean Breughel), Alfred Adam (the butcher), Louis Jouvet (the chaplain), Delphin (the dwarf)
Running time: 150 minutes (some American prints are up to one hour shorter)
Premiere: 3 December 1935, Marignan, Paris
16mm. Rental: Kit Parker, Corinth, Budget, Select, Em Gee Film Library

LE CRIME DE MONSIEUR LANGE (Films Obéron, 1935)
Director: Jean Renoir
Producer: André Halley des Fontaines
Assistant Directors: Pierre Prévert, Guy Darnoux
Screenplay: Jean Renoir, Jean Castanier, Jacques Prévert (dialogue)
Cinematographer: Jean Bachelet
Set Decoration: Jean Castanier, Robert Gys
Music: Jean Wiener, Joseph Kosma (song)
Sound: Guy Moreau, Louis Bogé
Editor: Marguerite Renoir
Cast: René Lefevre (M. Lange), Jules Berry (Batala), Florelle (Valentine), Nadia Sibirskaïa (Estelle), Sylvia Bataille (Edith), Maurice Baquet (Charles), Henri Guisol (Meunier)
Running time: 83 minutes
Premiere: 24 January 1936, Auber Palace, Paris
16mm. Rental: Audio Brandon

CRIME ET CHÂTIMENT (Général Production, 1935)
Director: Pierre Chenal
Screenplay: Pierre Chenal, Christian Stengel, Vladimir Strijewski, Marcel Aymé (dialogue), from Dostoievski's novel *Crime and Punishment* (1866)
Cinematographers: Colas, Joseph-Louis Mundwiller
Set Decoration: Aimé Bazin. The film utilizes the *mise-en-scène* of Gaston Baty for the Théâtre Montparnasse
Music: Arthur Honegger
Sound: Guy Moreau
Editor: André Galitzine
Cast: Harry Baur (Porphyre), Pierre Blanchar (Raskolnikov), Madeleine Ozeray (Sonia), Lucienne le Marchand (Dounia), Alexandre Rignault (Razoumikhine), Sylvie (Catherine Ivanova), Catherine Hessling (Elisabeth)
Running time: 110 minutes
16mm. Rental: Audio Brandon

PÉPÉ LE MOKO (Films-Paris-Production, 1936)
Director: Julien Duvivier
Producer: R. and R. Hakim
Assistant Director: Robert Vernay
Screenplay: Henri Jeanson, from Ashelbé's novel
Cinematographers: Jules Krüger, Marc Fossard
Set Decoration: Jacques Krauss
Music: Vincent Scotto, Mohammed Yguerbouchen
Sound: Antoine Archaimbaud
Editor: Marguerite Beaugé
Cast: Jean Gabin (Pépé le Moko), Mireille Balin (Gaby Gould), Lucas Gridoux (Inspector Slimane), Fernand Charpin (Régis), Line Noro (Inès), Fréhel (Tania), Saturnin Fabre (the grandfather), Gaston Modot (Jimmy)
Running time: 93 minutes
Premiere: 28 January 1937, Paris
16mm. Rental: Audio Brandon, Kit Parker, Budget, Select, Westcoast

CESAR (Films Marcel Pagnol, 1936)
Director and Producer: Marcel Pagnol
Assistant Director: Pierre Méré
Screenplay: Marcel Pagnol
Cinematographers: Willy, Willy-Gricha, Roger Ledru
Set Decoration: Marius Brouquier
Music: Vincent Scotto
Sound: Julien Coutellier, Banuls
Editors: Suzanne de Troye, Jeannette Ginestet
Cast: Raimu (César), Pierre Fresnay (Marius), Orane Demazis (Fanny), Fernand Charpin (Panisse), André Fouché (Césariot), Alida Rouffe (Honorine)
Running time: 121 minutes
Premiere: November 1936, César, Paris
16mm. Rental: Images, Budget, Kit Parker

MAYERLING (Concordia Production Cinématographique, Néro-Film, 1936)
Director: Anatole Litvak
Assistant Director: René Montis
Screenplay: Joseph Kessel, Irma von Cube, from Claude Anet's novel, *La Fin d'une idylle*
Set Decoration: Serge Pimenoff, André Andrejew, Robert Hubert
Costumes: Georges Annenkov
Music: Tchaikovsky, Weber, Johann Strauss, Arthur Honegger, Maurice Jaubert
Sound: William Sivel
Editor: Henri Rust
Cast: Charles Boyer (Rodolphe), Danielle Darrieux (Marie Vetsara), Jean Dax (Emperor François-Joseph), Marthe Regnier (Baroness Vetsara), Suzy Prim (Countess Larisch)
Running time: 90 minutes
16mm. Rental: Audio Brandon, Budget, Em Gee Film Library

LA GRANDE ILLUSION (R.A.C., 1937)
Director: Jean Renoir
Producer: Frank Rollmer, Albert Pinkovitch
Assistant Directors: Jacques Becker, Robert Rips
Screenplay: Jean Renoir, Charles Spaak
Cinematographers: Claude Renoir, Christian Matras, Yvan Bourguin, Earnest Bourreaud
Set Decoration: Eugene Lourié
Costumes: Decrais
Music: Joseph Kosma, Vincent Telly (lyrics)
Sound: Joseph de Bretagne
Editors: Marguerite Renoir, Marthe Huguet
Cast: Jean Gabin (Maréchal), Pierre Fresnay (Boieldieu), Erich von Stroheim (von Rauffenstein), Marcel Dalio (Rosenthal), Dita Parlo (Elsa), Julien Carette (the artist), Gaston Modot (the engineer), Jean Dasté (the teacher), Georges Peclet (a soldier), Jacques Becker (an English officer)

Running time: 112 minutes
Premiere: 4 June 1937, Marivaux, Paris
16mm. Rental: Images, Audio Brandon, Kit Parker, Budget, Video Communications, Classic Film Museum, Em Gee Film Library, Ivy, Institutional Cinema, Films Inc., Northwest Film Study Center, Select, Wholesome Film Center, Westcoast

REGAIN (Films Marcel Pagnol, 1937)
Director and Producer: Marcel Pagnol
Assistant Director: Léon Bourrely
Screenplay: Marcel Pagnol, from Jean Giono's novel, *Regain* (1930)
Cinematographers: Willy, Roger Ledru, Pierre Méré, Pierre Arnaudy, Henri Daries
Art Decoration: Marius Brouquier, René Paoletti
Music: Arthur Honegger
Sound: Jean Lecoq, Marcel Lavoignat, Max Olivier, Etienne Fabre
Editor: Suzanne de Troye, Jeanette Ginestet
Cast: Orane Demazis (Arsule), Fernandel (Urbain Gédémus), Gabriel Gabrio (Panturle), Robert Le Vigan (a policeman), Marguerite Moreno (La Mamèche)
Running time: 128 minutes
Premiere: October 1937, Marignan, Paris
16mm. Rental: Images

QUAI DES BRUMES (Ciné-Alliance, 1938)
Director: Marcel Carné
Producer: Grégoire Rabinovitch
Screenplay: Jacques Prévert, from Pierre Mac Orlan's novel, *Le Quai des brumes* (1927)
Cinematographers: Eugen Schüfftan, Louis Page, Marc Fossard, Pierre Alekan
Set Decoration: Alexandre Trauner
Music: Maurice Jaubert
Sound: Antoine Archaimbaud
Editor: René Le Hénaff
Cast: Jean Gabin (Jean), Michèle Morgan (Nelly), Marcel Simon (Zabel), Pierre Brasseur (Lucien), Edouard Delmont (Panama), Robert Le Vigan (the painter)
Running time: 90 minutes
Premiere: 18 May 1938, Marivaux, Paris
16mm. Rental: Budget

LA FEMME DU BOULANGER (Films Marcel Pagnol, 1938)
Director and Producer: Marcel Pagnol
Screenplay: Marcel Pagnol, from Jean Giono's novel, *Jean le bleu* (1932)
Cinematographers: Roger Ledru, Georges Benoit
Music: Vincent Scotto
Sound: Marcel Lavoignat
Editors: Suzanne de Troye, Marguerite Renoir, Suzanne Cabon
Cast: Raimu (Aimable), Fernand Charpin (the Marquis de Venelles), Ginette Leclerc (Aurélie), Alida Rouffe (Céleste), Charles Moulin (Dominique), Robert

Vattier (the priest), Edouard Delmont (Maillefer), Robert Bassac (the school-teacher)
Running time: 127 minutes
Premiere: September 1938, Marivaux, Paris
16mm. Rental: Images

LE JOUR SE LEVE (Productions Sigma, 1939)
Director: Marcel Carné
Assistant Directors: Pierre Blondy, Jean Fazy
Screenplay: Jacques Viot, Jacques Prévert
Cinematographers: Curt Courant, Philippe Agostini, André Bac
Set Decoration: Alexandre Trauner
Music: Maurice Jaubert
Sound: Armand Petitjean
Editor: René Le Hénaff
Cast: Jean Gabin (François), Jacqueline Laurent (Françoise), Jules Berry (Valentin), Arletty (Clara), Bernard Blier (Gaston)
Running time: 93 minutes
Premiere: 17 June 1939, Madeleine Cinéma, Paris
16mm. Rental: Kit Parker, Budget, Em Gee Film Library, Westcoast, Northwest Film Study Center

LA REGLE DU JEU (Nouvelle Edition Française, 1939)
Director and Producer: Jean Renoir
Assistant Directors: André Zwobada, Henri Cartier-Bresson
Screenplay: Jean Renoir, Carl Koch, Camille François
Cinematographers: Jean Bachelet, Jean-Paul Alphen, Alain Renoir
Set Decoration: Eugene Lourié, Max Douy
Costumes: Coco Chanel (dresses)
Music: Mozart, Monsigny, Sallabert, Johann Strauss, Saint-Saëns, Chopin, Vincent Scotto, Roger Desormières, Joseph Kosma (arrangements)
Sound: Joseph de Bretagne
Editor: Marguerite Renoir, Marthe Huguet
Cast: Marcel Dalio (the Marquis de la Chesnaye), Nora Gregor (Christine de la Chesnaye), Roland Toutain (André Jurieu), Jean Renoir (Octave), Paulette Dubost (Lisette), Gaston Modot (Schumacher), Julien Carette (Marceau)
Running time: 110 minutes
Premiere: 7 July 1939, Auber Palace, Colisée, Paris
16mm. Rental: Images, Audio Brandon, Kit Parker, Budget, Video Communications, Films Inc., Westcoast, Northwest Film Study Center

For the addresses of the various distributors, see *Film Programmers Guide to 16 mm. Rentals*, edited by Kathleen Weaver, 3d ed. (Albany, Calif.:Reel Research, 1980).

Index